DICTIONARY OF MILITARY

CW01023971

DICTIONARY OF MILITARY ABBREVIATIONS

BRITISH · EMPIRE · COMMONWEALTH

by **B. K. C. Scott,** B.A., A.L.A.

Tamarisk Books
Hastings, 1982

Copyright © 1982 by Brian Keith Colin Scott

First published 1982, by Tamarisk Books,
West Hill Cottage, Exmouth Place,
East Sussex, TN34 3JA

Printed by King Bros. & Potts Ltd.,
64-68 Norman Road, St. Leonards-on-Sea,
East Sussex

ISBN 0 907221 01 7

PREFACE

This book is intended to fill a need I discovered from my own experience in reading military history and collecting militaria. None of the general dictionaries of abbreviations I consulted contained a sufficiently large range of military abbreviations to answer all my questions, so I decided to compile my own.

I hope that both the collector and the researcher will find this work useful. It contains over 5000 abbreviations and acronyms used by and about the military forces of the United Kingdom, the Empire and Commonwealth, past and present, that may be found in official documents, on items of equipment, in military histories or contemporary accounts. In passing it also offers a reflection on the growth and complexity of military affairs as, although no limitation was set on the period to be covered, the majority of entries are from the nineteenth and twentieth centuries. The closing section of unofficial and alternative meanings preserves something of the serviceman's humour.

While a number of people, both friends and strangers, have helped with suggestions and contributions, and assistance has been gained from various libraries and museums, notably the IWM and NAM, any errors and omissions are my responsibility. Having said that, I would be pleased to hear from any reader who has information that would help to make a future edition more accurate and comprehensive.

B. K. C. Scott
November 1981

to the women
in my life

1/O	First Officer
2/IC	Second in Command
2Lt	Second Lieutenant
2/O	Second Officer
3/O	Third Officer
5BX	Five Basic Exercises
5 INNIS DG	Fifth Royal Inniskilling Dragoon Guards
A	Acting
	Admiral
AA	Aircraft Artificer
	Anti-Aircraft
	Army Act
	Assistant Adjutant
AAC	Anti-Aircraft Corps
	Army Air Corps
	Auxiliary Artillery Corps
AACC	Army Air Corps Centre
AACU	Anti-Aircraft Co-operation Unit
AADC	Air Aide-de-Camp
AAEE	Aircraft & Armament Experimental Establishment
AAEF	Australian Air Expeditionary Force
AAES	Anti-Aircraft Experimental Section
AAF	Allied Air Forces
	Auxiliary Air Force
A & AFA	Army & Air Force Act
AAFCE	Allied Air Forces Central Europe
AAFGL	Auxiliary Air Force General List
AAFNE	Allied Air Forces Northern Europe
AAFSE	Allied Air Forces Southern Europe
AAG	Assistant Adjutant-General
AAGW	Air-to-Air Guided Weapon
AAI	Allied Armies in Italy
AALD	Australian Army Legal Department
AAM	Air-to-Air Missile
AAMC	Australian Army Medical Corps
AAMS	Australian Army Medical Service
AAMWS	Australian Army Medical Women's Service
AANS	Australian Army Nursing Service
AAOC	Australian Army Ordnance Corps
AAOR	Anti-Aircraft Operations Room
AAQMG	Assistant Adjutant and Quartermaster-General
AAS	Air Armament School
AASC	Australian Army Service Corps
AASF	Advanced Air Striking Force
AATC	Anti-Aircraft Training Centre

AAU	Air Ambulance Unit
AAV	Ayrshire Artillery Volunteers
AAVC	Australian Army Veterinary Corps
AAWC	Australian Advisory War Council
AB	Able-Bodied Seaman
	Administrative Battalion
	Admiralty Board
	Air Board
	Army Book
ABCA	Army Bureau of Current Affairs
ABCD	Atomic-Biological-Chemical Defence
ABDACOM	American British Dutch Australian Command
ABM	Anti-Ballistic Missile
Abn	Airborne
ABRO	Army in Burma Reserve of Officers
ABS	Armoured Boarding Steamer
ABTU	Army Basic Training Unit
ABU	Administrative Base Unit
AC	Air Commodore
	Air Control
	Ambulance Corps
	Area Commander
	Army Circular
	Army Co-operation
	Army Corps
	Army Council
	Australian Cruiser
A/C	Aircraft
	Armoured Car
AC 1	Aircraftman 1st class
2	2nd class
ACA	Allied Control Commission for Austria
	Assistant Catering Accountant
ACAS(I)	Assistant Chief of the Air Staff (Intelligence)
(O)	(Operations)
(P)	(Policy)
(TR)	(Technical Requirements)
ACB	Airfield Construction Branch
ACC	Army Catering Corps
ACCHAN	Allied Command, Channel
ACD	Army Chaplains Department
A Cdre	Air Commodore
ACDS	Assistant Chief of Defence Staff
A Cdt	Air Commandant
ACE	Allied Command Europe

	Army Certificate of Education
ACF	Active Citizen Force
	African Colonial Forces
	Army Cadet Force
	Australian Comforts Fund
ACFA	Army Cadet Force Association
ACFS	Assistant Chief of Fleet Support
ACG	African Cavalry Guard
	Assistant Commissary-General
ACH	Aircrafthand
	Area Combined Headquarters
	Australian Commonwealth Horse
ACHQ	Area Combined Headquarters
ACHU	Aircrew Holding Unit
ACI	Air Council Instruction
	Army Council Instruction
ACIU	Allied Central Interpretation Unit
ACK	Assistant Cook
ACLANT	Allied Command, Atlantic
ACM	Air Chief Marshal
ACMF	Allied Central Mediterranean Force
	Australian Commonwealth Military Forces
ACMN	Aircrewman
ACNAS	Admiral Commanding North Atlantic Station
ACNS	Assistant Chief of Naval Staff
ACNS(A)	Assistant Chief of Naval Staff (Air)
ACO	Admiralty Compass Observatory
AC of N	Assistant Controller of the Navy
ACOS	Assistant Chief of Staff
ACP	After Conning Position
	Air Control Post
ACPL	Assistant Controller Personnel & Logistics
ACR	Admiral Commanding Reserves
	Air Control Radar
ACRO	Aircraft Control Room Officer
ACS	Aircraft Carrier Squadron
	Assistant Chief of Supplies
ACSEA	Allied Command South East Asia
AcSM	Academy Sergeant-Major
ACSRNAS	Armoured Car Section Royal Naval Air Service
A Ct	Air Commandant
ACT	Apparatus Carrier Telephone
ACV	Air-Cushion Vehicle
	Armoured Command Vehicle
ACW	Aircraftwoman
AD	Air Defence

3

	Aircraft Depot
	Air Despatch
	Artificer Diver
Ad	Administrative
ADA	Assistant Defence Advisor
ADATS	Assistant Director Auxiliary Territorial Service
ADAWS	Action Data Automation & Weapons System
	Assistant Director of Army Welfare Services
ADC	Aide-de-Camp
	Army Dental Corps
ADCC	Air Defence Cadet Corps
ADD	Airstream Direction Finder
	Armaments Design Department
ADDL	Airfield Dummy Deck Landing
ADEE	Air Defence Experimental Establishment
ADEM	Air Defences Eastern Mediterranean
ADFW	Assistant Director of Fortifications and Works
ADGB	Air Defence of Great Britain
ADGT	Assistant Director-General of Transportation
ADH	Assistant Director of Hygiene
ADI	Assistant Director of Intelligence
ADIZ	Air Defence Intercept Zone
ADJAG	Assistant Deputy Judge Advocate General
Adjt	Adjutant
Adjt-Gen	Adjutant-General
ADLR	Assistant Director of Light Railways
ADLS	Air Delivery Letter Service
ADM	Atomic Demolition Munitions
Adm	Admiral
ADME	Assistant Director of Mechanical Engineering
Adml	Admiral
ADMN	Administration
ADMS	Assistant Director of Medical Services
Admty	Admiralty
ADNA	Assistant Director of Naval Accounts
ADNC	Assistant Director of Naval Construction
ADNI	Assistant Director of Naval Intelligence
ADOC	Air Defence Operations Centre
ADOD	Assistant Director of Operations Division
ADOF	Assistant Director of Ordnance Factories
ADOS	Assistant Director of Ordnance Services
ADP	Air Defence Position
	Army Depot Police
	Assistant Director of Pathology
ADPS	Assistant Director Army Postal Services
ADRDE	Air Defence Research & Development Establishment

4

ADRT	Assistant Director of Railway Transport
ADS	Advanced Dressing Station
	Air Defence Ship
ADS & T	Assistant Director of Supplies & Transport
ADT	Advanced Driver Training
ADTn	Assistant Director of Transportation
Adv Gd	Advanced Guard
ADVRS	Assistant Director of Veterinary & Remount Services
ADVS	Assistant Director of Veterinary Services
AE	Aeronautical Engineer
	Air Efficiency Award
	Air Electronics
	Air Engineering
	Airframes & Engines
	Air Mechanic (Engines)
	Ammunition Examiner
	Armed Experimental
	Army Education
	Assault Engineer
	Assistant Engineer
AEAF	Allied Expeditionary Air Force
AEC	Army Educational Corps
AED	Air Equipment Department
AEDU	Admiralty Experimental Diving Unit
AEF	Air Experience Flight
	Allied Expeditionary Force
AEFLLC	Allied Expeditionary Force Long Lines Control
AEL	Admiralty Engineering Laboratory
AEOW	Air Engineer Officer's Writer
AEP	Army Equipment Policy
AER	Army Emergency Reserve
AEV	Armoured Engineer Vehicle
AEW	Admiralty Experimental Works
	Airborne Early Warning
AEWC	Airborne Early Warning & Control
AF	Admiral of the Fleet
	Air Force
	Army Form
A/F	Airfield
AFA	Air Force Act
AFAP	Air Forces Arabian Peninsula
AFC	Air Force Cross
	Australian Flying Corps
	Automatic Frequency Control
AFCE	Allied Forces Central Europe
AFCENT	Allied Forces Central Europe

AFCO	Admiralty Fleet Confidential Order
AFCS	Automatic Flight Control System
AFD	Admiralty Floating Dock
	Air Force Department
AFDC	Air Force Department Constabulary
AFDFS	Air Force Department Fire Service
AFDU	Air Fighting Development Unit
AFES	Admiralty Fuel Experimental Station
AFHQ	Allied Forces Headquarters
AFI	Auxiliary Force India
AFL	Air Force List
AFM	Air Force Medal
AFMC	Auxiliary Force Medical Corps
AFMED	Allied Forces Mediterranean
AFNE	Allied Forces Northern Europe
AFNORTH	Allied Forces Northern Europe
AFO	Admiralty Fleet Order
	Army Forwarding Officer
AFOR	Air Force Operations Room
AFPS	Army Film & Photographic Section
AFPU	Army Film & Photographic Unit
AFS	Advanced Flying School
	Army Fire Service
AFSE	Allied Forces Southern Europe
AFSOUTH	Allied Forces Southern Europe
AFTCC	Air Force Troop Carrier Command
AFU	Advanced Flying Unit
	Assault Fire Unit
AFV	Armoured Fighting Vehicle
AFVC	Auxiliary Force Veterinary Corps
AFW	Army Field Workshop
AG	Adjutant-General
	Air Gunner
	Army Group
A/G	Anti-Gas
AGC	Amphibious Group Command
AGE	Admiralty Gunnery Establishment
AGF	Adjutant/General to the Forces
AGH	Australian General Hospital
AGI	Air Gunnery Instructor
A/GI	Anti-Gas Instructor
AGL(T)	Automatic Gunlaying (Turret)
AGL(T)TRG	Automated Gun Laying (Turret) Training
AGM	Admiralty General Message
	Air-to-Ground Missile
AGRA	Army Group Royal Artillery

AGRM	Adjutant-General Royal Marines
AGS	Automatic Gain Stabilization
AH	Aircraft Handler
	Army Helicopter
AHB	Air Historical Branch
AHC	Army Hospital Corps
AHQ	Air Headquarters
	Army Headquarters
AI	Admiralty Instruction
	Air Intelligence
	Airborne Interception
AIA	Assistant Inspector of Armourers
AIB	Admiralty Interview Board
AIC	Australian Intelligence Corps
AID	Aeronautical Inspection Department
AIF	Australian Imperial Force
AIG	Assistant Instructor in Gunnery
AIL	Air Intelligence Liaison
AILO	Air Intelligence Liaison Officer
AIP	Allied Intelligence Publication
AIY	Ayrshire Imperial Yeomanry
A/J	Anti-Jamming
AJAG	Assistant Judge Advocate General
AKC	Army Kinematograph Corporation
AL	Admiralty Letter
	Air Electrical
	Army List
A/L	Air-Landing
ALC	Army Legal Corps
ALCM	Air-Launched Cruise Missile
ALEX	Alert Exercise
ALFCE	Allied Land Forces Central Europe
ALFSEA	Allied Land Forces South-East Asia
ALG	Advanced Landing Ground
ALH	Australian Light Horse
ALLA	Allied Long Lines Agency
ALMAJCOM	All Major Commands
ALO	Air Liaison Officer
ALOW	Air Electrical Officer's Writer
AM	Air Marshal
	Air Ministry
	Army Manual
	Auxiliary Minesweeper
AMA	Army Mounteering Association
AMACAB	Allied Military Administration Civil Affairs Branch
AMB	Admiralty Medical Board

	Air Ministry Bulletin
	Armoured Motor Battery
AMC	Air Ministry Constabulary
	Air Mounting Centre
	Army Medical Corps
	Auxiliary Minesweeper Coastal
AMD	Army Medical Department
AMDP	Air Member for Development & Production
AMEE	Admiralty Marine Engineering Establishment
AMES	Air Ministry Experimental Station
AMETS	Army Meteorological System
AMF	Allied Command Europe Mobile Force
	Australian Military Forces
AMG	Allied Military Government
AMGO	Assistant Master-General of Ordnance
AMGOT	Allied Military Government Occupied Territories
AMI	Auxiliary Minesweeper Inshore
AMIC	Army Methods of Instruction Centre
AMLO	Assistant Military Landing Officer
AMN	Aircraft Mechanician
Amn	Ammunition
AMO	Admiralty Monthly Order
	Air Ministry Order
AMP	Air Member for Personnel
	Assisted Maintenance Period
AMPC	Auxiliary Military Pioneer Corps
AMR	Auckland Mounted Rifles
AMRD	Aircraft Maintenance & Repair Department
	Air Member for Research & Development
AMRE	Air Ministry Research Establishment
AMS	Army Map Service
	Army Medical Service
	Army Medical Staff
	Assistant Military Secretary
	Auxiliary Minesweeper
AMSEF .	Anti-Minesweeping Explosive Float
AMSIS	Air Ministry Secret Intelligence Summary
AMSO	Air Member for Supply & Organization
AMT	Air Member for Training
AMTRAC	Amphibious Tractor
AMW	Air Ministry Warden
ANA	Assistant Naval Attache
ANC	Area Naval Commander
ANCA	Allied Naval Communications Agency
ANCXF	Allied Naval Commander Expeditionary Force
ANF	Atlantic Nuclear Force

8

ANFO	Ammonium Nitrate/Fuel Oil
ANGLICO	Air & Naval Gunfire Liaison Company
ANHC	Army Native Hospital Corps
ANMI	Allied Naval Manoeuvring Instructions
ANS	Advanced Navigation School
	Air Navigation School
ANXF	Allied Naval Expeditionary Force
ANZAC	Australian & New Zealand Army Corps
AO	Air Ordnance
	Army Order
AOBS	Army Outward Bound School
AOC	Air Officer Commanding
	Army Ordnance Corps
AOC-in-C	Air Officer Commanding-in-Chief
AOD	Advanced Ordnance Depot
	Army Ordnance Department
AOER	Army Officers Emergency Reserve
AOME	Assistant Ordnance Mechanical Engineer
AOO	Amphibious Operations Officer
AOP	Air Observation Post
	Army Observation Post
	Artillery Observation Post
AOPF	Air Observation Post Flight
AORG	Army Operational Research Group
AOS	Air Observer School
AOTD	Air Organisation & Training Division
AOW	Army Ordnance Workshop
AP	Aiming Point
	Air Publication
	Armour-Piercing
	Assistant Paymaster
	Auxiliary Patrol
APA	Army Parachute Association
	Auxiliary Personnel Attack
APC	Armament Practice Camp
	Armoured Personnel Carrier
	Armour-Piercing, Capped
	Army Pay Corps
APCBC	Armour-Piercing, Capped, Ballistic Capped
APCR	Armour-Piercing Composite Rigid
APCT	Armour-Piercing, Capped, Tracer
APD	Admiralty Press Division
	Army Pay Department
	Auxiliary Personnel Destroyer
APDS	Armour-Piercing Discarding Sabot
APDS-T	Armour-Piercing Discarding Sabot Tracer

APFSDS	Armour-Piercing Fin Stabilised Discarding Sabot
APHE	Armour-Piercing High Explosive
API	Armour-Piercing Incendiary
APIS	Army Photographic Interpretation Section
API-T	Armour-Piercing Incendiary Tracer
APJI	Assistant Parachute Jump Instructor
APL	Aden Protectorate Levies
APM	Assistant Paymaster
	Assistant Provost Marshal
APO	Acting Pilot Officer
	Army Post Office
APOAM	Acting Petty Officer Air Mechanic
APOC	Army Post Office Corps
App	Apprentice
APS	Armament Practice Station
APSE	Armour-Piercing Secondary Effects
APSO	Assistant Polaris Systems Officer
AP & SS	Army Printing & Stationery Service
APT	Airportable
AP-T	Armour-Piercing Tracer
APTC	Army Physical Training Corps
APTS	Army Physical Training Staff
AQMG	Assistant Quartermaster-General
AQMS	Artificer Quartermaster-Sergeant
AR	Adelaide Rifles
	Air Radio
ARA	Army Rifle Association
ARB	Auxiliary Repair Battle Damage
ARC	Aircrew Reception Centre
ARD	Armaments Research Department
ARDE	Armament Research & Development Establishment
ARFA	Allied Radio Frequency Agency
ARFCOS	Armed Forces Courier Service
ARI	Airborne Radio Installation
ARL	Admiralty Research Laboratory
Armd	Armoured
ARMN	Airman
Armt	Armament
ARNO	Association of Retired Naval Officers
ARP	Air Raid Precautions
	Ammunition Refilling Point
ARR	Australian Rifle Regiment
ARRCS	Air-Raid Reporting Control Ship
ARRE	Assault Regiment Royal Engineers
ARS	Advanced Regulating Station
	Army Radio School

ART	Artillery
Art	Artificer
ARTO	Area Railway Transport Officer
ARV	Armoured Recovery Vehicle
AS	Admiral Superintendent
	Air Steward
	Air Support
	Air-to-Surface
	Assault Squadron
A/S	Anti-Submarine
ASA	Appropriate Superior Authority
	Army Ski Association
	Assistant Stores Accountant
ASC	Air Support Control
	Army Selection Centre
	Army Service Corps
ASCB	Army Sports Control Board
ASD	Admiralty Salvage Department
	Anti-Submarine Division
	Armament Supply Department
	Army Schools Department
ASDIC	Allied Submarine Detection Investigation Committee
ASE	Admiralty Signals Establishment
	Allied Supplies Executive
A & SH	Argyll & Sutherland Highlanders
ASI	Air Speed Indicator
	Arctic Survival Instructor
ASJR	Army Summary Jurisdiction Regulations
ASL	Acting Sub-Lieutenant
ASM	Air-to-Surface Missile
ASN	Army Service Number
	Air Staff Officer
ASO	Armament Supply Officer
	Assistant Section Officer
ASOC	Air Support Operations Centre
ASP	Air Stores Park
	Ammunition Sub-Park
	Anti-Submarine Patrol
ASR	Air-Sea Rescue
	Army Scripture Reader
ASRE	Admiralty Signals and Radar Establishment
ASRF	Air-Sea Rescue Flight
ASROC	Anti-Submarine Rocket
ASRS	Air-Sea Rescue Service
ASTD	Assistant Steward
ASU	Aircraft Storage Unit

ASV	Air to Surface Vessel
ASW	Anti-Submarine Warfare
	Anti-Submarine Weapon
ASWE	Admiralty Surface-Weapons Establishment
ASWEX	Anti-Submarine Warfare Exercise
ASWGW	Anti-Submarine Wire-Guided Weapon
ASWI	Anti-Submarine Warfare Installations
ASWLR	Anti-Submarine Warning, Long Range
ASWRC	Anti-Submarine Warfare Research Centre
AT	Aircraft Technician
	Air Transport
	Ammunition Technician
	Anti-Tank
	Army Transport
A/T	Anti-Torpedo
ATA	Air Transport Auxiliary
	Army Temperance Association
ATAF	Allied Tactical Air Force
ATAR	Anti-Tank Aircraft Rocket
ATC	Air Traffic Control
	Air Training Corps
	Anti-Torpedo Craft
ATCA	Allied Tactical Communications Agency
ATFERO	Atlantic Ferry Organisation
ATGW	Anti-Tank Guided Weapon
A/Tk	Anti-Tank
ATO	Accelerated Take-Off
	Ammunition Technical Officer
ATRI	Air Transportable Radio Installation
ATS	Army Technical School
	Auxiliary Territorial Service
ATURM	Amphibious Training Unit Royal Marines
AUM	Air-to-Underwater Missile
AUWE	Admiralty Underwater Weapons Establishment
AV	Artillery Volunteers
AVC	Aireworth Volunteer Corps
	Army Veterinary Corps
AVD	Army Veterinary Department
AVGAS	Aviation Gasoline
AVLB	Armoured Vehicle Launched Bridge
AVLH	Assam Valley Light Horse
AVM	Air Vice-Marshal
AVO	Administrative Veterinary Officer
AVR	Armoured Vehicle, Reconnaissance
	Army Volunteer Reserve
AVRE	Armoured Vehicle Royal Engineers

AVRS	Army Veterinary Remount Service
AW	Air Weapon
	Amphibious Warfare
	Armstrong Whitworth
AWACS	Airborne Warning and Control System
AWAS	Australian Women's Army Service
AWC	Air Warfare Co-ordination
AWD	Air Warfare Division
AWDATS	Artillery Weapon Data Transmission System
AWHA	Australian Women's Home Army
AWI	Air Warfare Instructor
AWL	Absent Without Leave
AWO	Admiralty Weekly Order
AWOL	Absent Without Leave
AWSOS	Army Women's Services Officers School
AWT	Arctic Warfare Training
AWTR	Assistant Writer
AY	Ayrshire Yeomanry
B	Boatswain
	Bomber
	Bugler
BA	Bolt Action
B/A	Bomb-Aimer
BAAG	British Army Aid Group
BABS	Beam Approach Beacon System
BAD	British Admiralty Delegation
BAFF	British Air Forces in France
BAFG	British Air Forces in Greece
BAFO	British Air Forces of Occupation
	British Army Forces Overseas
BAFSV	British Armed Forces Special Vouchers
BAGS	Bombing and Gunnery School
BALTAP	Baltic Approaches
BAMA	British Army Motoring Association
BAMS	British American Minesweeper
BANEWS	British Army News Service
BANHC	Bengal Army Native Hospital Corps
BAO	British Army of Occupation
BAOR	British Army of the Rhine
BAPO	British Army Post Office
BAPT	Basic Avionics Procedure Trainer
BAR	Browning Automatic Rifle
BARV	Beach Armoured Recovery Vehicle
BAS	British Army Staff
BASO	Brigade Air Support Officer

BAT	Battalion Anti-Tank
	Beam Approach Training
	Blind Approach Technique
Bat	Battalion
	Battery
BATES	Battlefield Artillery Target Engagement System
BATF	Beam Approach Training Flight
BATM	British Admiralty Technical Mission
Batn	Battalion
Batt	Battalion
	Battery
BATUS	British Army Training Unit Suffield
BAU	Bombing Analysis Unit
BB	Balloon Barrage
BBG	[Governor's] Bodyguard Bombay
BBRM	British Bombing Research Mission
BBSU	British Bombing Survey Unit
BC	Bad Conduct
	Battery Commander
	Battle-Cruiser
	Bengal Cavalry
	Bombay Cavalry
	Bomber Command
BCATP	British Commonwealth Air Training Plan
BCEL	British Commonwealth Ex-services League
BCF	Battle Cruiser Force
BCFK	British Commonwealth Forces Korea
BCH	Bomber Command Headquarters
BCIR	Bomber Command Intelligence Report
BCIS	Bomber Command Intelligence Summary
BCKB	British Commonwealth Korean Base
B Cmd	Bomber Command
BCOF	British Commonwealth Occupation Force
BCOO	Bomber Command Operation Order
BCS	Battle Cruiser Squadron
BCTPC	Bomber Command Tactical Planning Committee
BD	Barrack Department
	Battle Dress
	Bomb Disposal
	Boom Defence
Bd/Cpl	Band Corporal
Bd/CSgt	Band Colour Sergeant
BDD	Boom Defence Depot
Bde	Brigade
BDO	Boom Defence Officer
Bdr	Bombardier

BDS	Bomb Damage Survey
	Bomb Disposal Squad
	British Defence Staff
Bd/Sgt	Band Sergeant
BDTF	Bomber Defence Training Flight
BDU	Bomb Disposal Unit
	Bombing Development Unit
BDV	Boom Defence Vessel
BE	Bleriot Experimental
B/E	Boy Entrant
BEF	British Expeditionary Force
BEM	British Empire Medal
BEME	Brigade Electrical & Mechanical Engineer
BETFOR	British Element Trieste Force
BF	Bayonet Fighting
	Bengal Fusiliers
	Breadalbane Fencibles
	Bristol Fighter
	British Forces
BFA	[Category] B Flying Accident
BFAP	British Forces Arabian Peninsula
BFBS	British Forces Broadcasting Service
BFF	Burma Frontier Force
BFG	British Forces Germany
BFH	British Field Hospital
BFL	British Foreign Legion
BFPO	British Forces Post Office
BF Set	British Field [Wireless] Set
BFT	Basic Fitness Test
BG	Battle Group
	Bren Gun(ner)
	Brigade of Gurkhas
BGB	[Governor's] Bodyguard Bengal
BGC	Bren Gun Carrier
Bgde	Brigade
B Gen	Brigadier-General
B & GF	Bombing & Gunnery Flight
BGMA	British Guiana Militia Artillery
BGS	Bombing & Gunnery School
	Brigadier General Staff
BGVF	British Guiana Volunteer Force
BH	Base Hospital
BHA	Bengal Horse Artillery
	Bombay Horse Artillery
BHQ	Battalion Headquarters
	Brigade Headquarters

B(I)	Bomber (Intruder)
BI(A)R	Board of Inquiry (Army) Rules
BIO	Bengal Irregular Cavalry
BID	Blockade Intelligence Department
BIO	Brigade Intelligence Officer
BIOS	British Intelligence Objectives Sub-committee
BIY	Bedfordshire Imperial Yeomanry
BJCB	British Joint Communication Board
BJSM	British Joint Services Mission
BL	Bengal Lancers
	Breech-Loading
	British Legion
	Bundelkund Legion
B/L	Bridgelayer
BLA	British Liberation Army
BLAV	British Latin America Volunteers
BLC	Bengal Light Cavalry
	Bombay Light Cavalry
BLEU	Blind Landing Experimental Unit
BLH	Bihar Light Horse
BLO	Bombardment Liaison Officer
BLP	Backloading Point
BLR	Beyond Local Repair
	Breech-Loading Rifle
BLT	Battalion Landing Team
BM	Boatswain's Mate
	Boilermaker
	Brigade Major
bm	breech mechanism
BMA	Brigade Maintenance Area
	British Military Administration
	British Military Authority
BMD	Bengal Medical Department
BMDO	Bomb & Mine Disposal Officer
BMEWS	Ballistic Missile Early Warning System
BMH	British Military Hospital
BMM	British Military Mission
BMP	Burma Military Police
BMR	Bihar Mounted Rifles
	Border Mounted Rifles
BN	Blind Navigation
Bn	Battalion
BNA	British Naval Attache
BNAF	British North Africa Force
BNCO	British Non-Commissioned Officer
Bndr	Bandmaster

BNGM	British Naval Gunnery Mission
BNI	Bengal Native Infantry
BNRVR	Bengal-Nagpore Railway Volunteer Rifles
BNS	British Naval Staff
B & NW RY BN	Bengal & North-Western Railway Battalion
BO	Battalion Orders
	Board of Ordnance
	British Officer
BOD	Base Ordnance Depot
Bomb	Bombardier
Bomb SC	Bombay Staff Corps
B Ops	Bomber Operations
BOR	Battalion Orderly Room
	British Other Rank
BOW	Base Ordnance Workshop
BOWO	Brigade Ordnance Warrant Officer
BPB	Boom Patrol Boat
BPC	Beach Patrol Craft
BPF	British Pacific Fleet
BPMH	Brompton Park Military Hospital
BPSO	Base Personnel Staff Officer
BPT	Battle-Practice Target
BQMS	Battery Quartermaster-Sergeant
BR	Birmingham Repair
	Book of Reference
Br	Bombardier
	Brigadier
	Bugler
BRA	Bombing Restriction Area
	Brigadier, Royal Artillery
Br Coy	Bearer Company
BRD	Base Remount Depot
Bren	BRno/ENfield
Brev	Brevet
Brig	Brigadier
Brig-Gen	Brigadier-General
BRNC	Britannia Royal Naval College
BS	Battle Squadron
	Bomber Support
	Border Scouts
BSA	Birmingham Small Arms
BSAP	British South Africa Police
BSC	Bengal Staff Corps
	British Security Co-ordination
BSDU	Bomber Support Development Unit
BSF	British Salonika Force

17

BSM	Battery Sergeant-Major
B & SV	Barkston Ashe & Skyrac Volunteers
BT	Bomber Transport
Bt	Brevet
BTA	British Troops in Austria
BTE	British Troops in Egypt
BTG	British Troops in Germany
BTI	British Troops in Iraq
BTIC	Bomb Targets Information Committee
BTNA	British Troops in North Africa
BTO	Battalion Transport Officer
BTS	Boys Technical School
Bty	Battery
BUCO	Build-Up Control Organisation
BVC	Bushveldt Carbineers
BVLA	British Volunteers Latin America
BVR	Bangalore Volunteer Rifles
BW	Barrack Warden
	Biological Warfare
	Black Watch
B & W Dgns	Berkshire & Westminster Dragoons
BWO	Bridge Wireless Officer
BWSC	British War Supplies Committee
BY	Bedfordshire Yeomanry
BYC	Bengal Yeomanry Cavalry
	Berkshire Yeomanry Cavalry
BVCH	Buckinghamshire Yeomanry Cavalry Hussars
BYMS	British Yard Minesweepers
C	Cadet
	Canada
	Cavalry
	Communication
	Cook
CA	Canadian Army
	Caterer
	Catering Accountant
	Clothing Allowance
	Coast Artillery
	Colonial Allowance
	Control Armourer
	Corps Adjutant
CAA	Chief Aircraft Artificer
CAACU	Civilian Anti-Aircraft Co-operation Unit
CAAEE	Coast & Anti-Aircraft Experimental Establishment
CAAIS	Computer Assisted Action Information System

CAATO	Combined Army Air Transport Organisation
CAC	Canadian Armoured Corps
CADC	Canadian Army Dental Corps
CAEU	Casualty Air Evacuation Unit
CAF	Canadian Armed Forces
	Chief Air Fitter
CAFG	Commander Air Forces Gulf
CAFO	Confidential Admiralty Fleet Order
	Confidential Air Force Order
CAG	Civil Air Guard
Cal	Calibre
CALE	Canadian Army Liaison Executive
CAMC	Canadian Army Medical Corps
CAMD	Craft & Amphibious Material Department
CAMN	Chief Aircraft Mechanician
CAM Ship	Catapult Aircraft Merchant Ship
CAORG	Canadian Army Operational Research Group
CAP	Combat Air Patrol
	Contingency Amphibious Plan
CAPC	Canadian Army Pay Corps
CAPO	Canadian Army Post Office
Capt	Captain
Capt-Gen	Captain-General
CAR	Central African Regiment
CAS	Chief of Air Staff
	Coast Artillery School
CASC	Canadian Army Service Corps
	Ceylon Army Service Corps
CATC	Coast Artillery Training Centre
CATOR	Combined Air Transport Operations Room
Cav	Cavalry
CAVC	Canadian Army Veterinary Corps
CB	Cadet Battalion
	Cavalry Brigade
	Confidential Book(s)
	Confined (Confinement) to Barracks
	Counter Bombardment
CBE	Central Bomber Establishment
CBFAP	Commander British Forces Arabian Peninsula
CBFCA	Commander, British Forces Caribbean Area
CBFG	Commander, British Forces Gulf
CBME	Combined Bureau Middle East
CBNS	Commander, British Naval Staff
CBO	Combined Bomber Offensive
	Counter-Battery Officer
CBR	Chemical-Biological-Radiological

CBU	Cluster Bomb Unit
CBW	Chemical & Biological Warfare
CC	Cadet Corps
	Cape Corps
	Coastal Command
	Combat Clothing
	Corps Commander
CCA	Carrier-Controlled Approach
CCAC	Canadian Casualty Assembly Centre
CCATS	Chief Controller Auxiliary Territorial Service
	Controller Commandant Auxiliary Territorial Service
CCBS	Commodore, Contract-Built Ships
CCC	Combat Cargo Command
CCCC	Cape Colony Cyclist Corps
CCD	Commander of Coast Defences
CCDU	Coastal Command Development Unit
CCEA	Chief Control Electrical Artificer
CCEL	Chief Control Electrician
CCEMN	Chief Control Electrical Mechanician
CCF	Captain, Coastal Forces
	Combined Cadet Force
CCFA	Combined Cadet Force Association
CCFATU	Coastal Command Fighter Affiliation Training Unit
CCFIS	Coastal Command Flying Instructors School
CCG	Control Commission for Germany
CCIS	Command & Control Information System
C Cmd	Coastal Command
CCMF	The Churches' Committee for Supplementing Religious Education Among Men in H.M. Forces
CCMP	Ceylon Corps of Military Police
CCO	Chief of Combined Operations
CCOS	Combined Chiefs of Staff
CCRA	Commander, Corps of Royal Artillery
CCS	Casualty Clearing Station
	Combined Chiefs of Staff
CCTA	Council of County Territorial Associations
CCTF	Combat Cargo Task Force
CCY	Chief Communications Yeoman
CD	Canadian Forces Decoration
	Captain of the Dockyard
	Civil Defence
	Clearance Diver
	Coast Defence
	Compass Department
Cd	Commissioned
CDB	Combat Development Board

CDCN	Controller Defence Communications Network
CDEE	Chemical Defence Experimental Establishment
CDES	Chemical Defence Experimental Station
CDF	Civil Defence Force
CDL	Civil Defence Legion
	Canal Defence Light
C & DM RGA	Cornwall & Devon Miners Royal Garrison Artillery
Cdo	Commando
Cdr	Commander
CDRA	Corps of Drivers Royal Artillery
CDRE	Chemical Defence Research Establishment
Cdre	Commodore
CDS	Chief of Defence Staff
Cdt	Cadet
CE	Canadian Engineers
	Chief Engineer
	Control Electrician
CEA	Chief Electrical Artificer
	Control Electrical Artificer
CEAD	Chief Engineer & Superintendent of Armaments Design
CEF	Canadian Expeditionary Force
CEFO	Complete Equipment Fighting Order
CEG	Career Employment Group
CEL(A)	Chief Electrician (Air)
(AW)	(Air Weapon)
CELMN	Chief Electrical Mechanician
CEM	Captured Enemy Material
	Control Electrical Mechanic
CEMN	Control Electrical Mechanician
CENTAG	Central Army Group
CENTO	Central Treaty Organisation
CEOA	Central European Operating Agency
CEP	Circular Error Probability
CEPC	Chief Engineer Port Construction
CEPS	Central European Pipeline System
CERA	Chief Engine Room Artificer
CESSAC	Church of England Soldiers' Sailors' & Airmen's Clubs
CET	Combat Engineering Tractor
CF	Chaplain to the Forces
CFA	Canadian Field Artillery
	Cape Field Artillery
CFC	Canadian Forestry Corps
CFE	Central Fighter Establishment
CFI	Chief Flying Instructor
CFM	Cadet Forces Medal
Cfn	Craftsman

CFPS	Captain, Fishery Protection Squadron
CFS	Central Flying School
Cftn	Craftsman
CG	Captain of Gun
	Captain of the Guard
	Coldstream Guards
	Commandant General
	Commissary-General
	Cruiser-Guided-missile.
CGA	Canadian Garrison Artillery
	Cape Garrison Artillery
CGC	Cruiser, Guided-missile & Command
CGH	Cape of Good Hope Decoration
CGI	Chief Ground Instructor
	Chief Gunnery Instructor
	Corrugated Galvanised Iron
CGM	Conspicuous Gallantry Medal
CGR	Canadian Garrison Regiment
CGRM	Commandant General Royal Marines
CGS	Central Gliding School
	Central Gunnery School
	Chief of the General Staff
CH	Chain Home
Ch	Chaplain
Ch E	Chief Engineer
CHEL	Chain Home Extra Low
Ch F	Chaplain of the Fleet
CHL	Chain Home Low
CHQ	Company Headquarters
Ch Skr	Chief Skipper
CHMP	Chan Hills Military Police
CIA	Chief Inspector of Armaments
CIB	Canadian Infantry Brigade
CIBG	Canadian Infantry Brigade Group
CIC	Canadian Intelligence Corps
	Combat Information Centre
	Combined Intelligence Committee
	Counter-Intelligence Corps
CICI	Combined Intelligence Centre Iraq
CID	Committee of Imperial Defence
CIESS	Chief Inspector of Engineer & Signal Stores
CIGS	Chief of the Imperial General Staff
CIH	Central India Horse
C-in-C	Commander-in-Chief
CINCEASTLANT	Commander-in-Chief Eastern Atlantic
CINCENT	Commander-in-Chief Allied Forces Central Europe

CINCFLT	Commander-in-Chief, Fleet
CINCHAN	Commander-in-Chief Channel & Southern North Sea
CINCHF	Commander-in-Chief, Home Fleet
CINCIBER-LANT	Commander-in-Chief Iberian Atlantic Area
CINCMAIR-CHAN	Commander-in-Chief, Allied Maritime Air, Channel
CINCMED	Commander-in-Chief, Mediterranean
CINCNORTH	Commander-in-Chief, Allied Forces, Northern Europe
CINCSOUTH	Commander-in-Chief, Allied Forces, Southern Europe
CINCWA	Commander-in-Chief Western Approaches
CINCWEST-LANT	Commander-in-Chief, Western Atlantic
CINO	Chief Inspector of Naval Ordnance
CIOS	Combined Intelligence Objectives Sub-committee
CIPC	Combined Intelligence Priorities Committee
CIRES	Chief Inspector of Royal Engineer Stores
CIST	Chief Inspector of Supplementary Transport
CIU	Central Interpretation Unit
CIV	Central Inspectorate of Vehicles
	City Imperial Volunteers
CJCB	Commonwealth Joint Communication Board
Ck	Cook
Ck L	Cookery Officer
CL	Cliff Leader
	Communication Lieutenant
	Cruiser, Light
CLAA	Cruiser, Light, Anti-Aircraft
CLCR	Communication Lieutenant-Commander
CLE	City of London Engineers
CLF	Commander Land Forces
CLG	Cruiser, Light, Guided-missile
CLH	Calcutta Light Horse
CLI	Cornwall Light Infantry
CLNG	City of London National Guard
CLR	City of London Rifles
CLRV	County of London Regiment [Volunteers]
CLY	County of London Yeomanry
CM	Command Money
	Controlled Mining
	Court Martial
	Cruise Missile
C & M	Care & Maintenance
CMA	Controller Military Accounts
	Corps Maintenance Area
	Corps of Military Accountants

CMAA	Courts-Martial (Appeals) Act
CMAB	Combined Munitions Assignments Board
CMAC	Courts-Martial Appeal Court
CMAR	Courts-Martial Appeal Rules
CMB	Chief Motor Boatman
	Coastal Motor Boat
Cmd	Command
Cmdg	Commanding
Cmdr	Commander
Cmdre	Commodore
Cmdt	Commandant
Cmdt Gen	Commandant General
CME	Chief Mechanical Engineer
CMEA	Chief Marine Engineering Artificer
CMEM	Chief Marine Engineering Mechanic
CMF	Central Mediterranean Force
	Citizens Military Forces
CMGC	Canadian Machine Gun Corps
Cm Gds	Coldstream Guards
CMHQ	Canadian Military Headquarters
CMP	Camp Military Police
	Canadian Military Pattern
	Corps of Military Police
CMPC	Canadian Military Police Corps
CMP(I)	Corps of Military Police (India)
CMM	Chief Motor Mechanic
CMMGB	Canadian Motor Machine Gun Brigade
CMMP	Corps of Military Mounted Police
CMR	Canadian Mounted Rifles
	Cape Mounted Rifles
CMRGA	Ceylon & Mauritius Royal Garrison Artillery
CMSC	Cape Medical Staff Corps
CMT	Chief Medical Technician
CMVS	Cavalry Mobile Veterinary Section
CMY	Cape Mounted Yeomanry
CNA	Cadets Norfolk Artillery
CNAS	Chief of Naval Air Services
CNEO	Chief Naval Engineer Officer
CNI	Chief of Naval Information
CNJA	Chief Naval Judge Advocate
CNOCS	Captain Naval Operations Command Systems
CNR	Chief Naval Representative
CN Regt	Chota Nagpur Regiment
CNS	Chief of the Naval Staff
CNSSO	Chief Naval Supply & Secretariat Officer
CO	Chief Officer

	Commanding Officer
	Communication Officer
	Conscientious Objector
Co	Company
COA	Corps of Ordnance Artificers
COAC	Commanding Officer Atlantic Coast
CODAG	Combined Diesel and/or Gas-turbine
CODC	Combined Operations Development Centre
CODOG	Combined Diesel or Gas-turbine
COEA	Chief Ordnance Electrical Artificer
COEL	Chief Ordnance Electrician
COEMN	Chief Ordnance Electrical Mechanician
COEW	Combined Operations Experimental Wing
COF	Captain Of the Fleet
C of A	Corps of Armourers
C of F	Chaplain of the Fleet
C of N	Controller of the Navy
C of S Ch	Church of Scotland Chaplain
COH	Corporal of Horse
COHQ	Combined Operations Headquarters
COL	Chain Overseas Low
Col	Colonel
Col Sgt	Colour Sergeant
Coln	Column
Com	Commander
	Commodore
COMAF	Commodore Amphibious Forces
Comd	Command
Comdr	Commander
Comdt	Commandant
COME	Chief Officer Mechanical Engineering
	Chief Ordnance Mechanical Engineer
Com-Gen	Commissary-General
Compy	Company
COMZONE	Communication Zone
Con	Constructor
CONVEX	Convoy Exercise
COO	Chief Ordnance Officer
COPC	Combined Operational Planning Committee
COPP	Combined Operations Pilotage Party
COREP	Combined Operations Repair Organization
Corp	Corporal
Corpl	Corporal
COS	Chiefs of Staff
COSAG	Combined Steam And/or Gas-turbine
COSD	Command Supply Depot

COSSAC	Chief of Staff to the Supreme Allied Commander
COTC	Canadian Officers Training Corps
COW	Coventry Ordnance Works
Coxn	Coxswain
Coy	Company
CP	Civil Power
	Climate Pay
	Command Paymaster
CPASC	Canadian Permanent Army Service Corps
CPAV	Cinque Ports Artillery Volunteers
CPD	Contract & Purchase Department
	Controller of Projectile Development
CPE	Chief Polaris Executive
CPI	Corps of Permanent Instructors
Cpl	Corporal
CPLMB	Chief Plumber
CPO	Chief Petty Officer
CPOACMN	Chief Petty Officer Aircrewman
CPOCA	Chief Petty Caterer
CPOCK	Chief Petty Officer Cook
CPOMA	Chief Petty Officer Medical Assistant
CPOPT	Chief Petty Officer Physical Trainer
CPOSA	Chief Petty Officer Stores Accountant
CPOSTD	Chief Petty Officer Steward
CPOWTR	Chief Petty Officer Writer
CPR	Cape Peninsular Rifles
	Clerk (Pay & Records)
CPRV	Cinque Ports Rifle Volunteers
CPSC	Canadian Permanent Signal Corps
CPV	Command Post Vehicle
CQB	Close-Quarter Battle
CQMS	Camp Quartermasters Store
	Company Quartermaster Sergeant
CR	Control Rating
Cr	Commander
	Cruiser
CRA	Commander Royal Artillery
CRAA	Commander-At-Arms
CRAC	Commander Royal Armoured Corps
CRASC	Commander Royal Army Service Corps
CRB	Chemical-Radiological-Biological [Warfare]
CRC	Control & Reporting Centre
CRCE	Chief Railway Construction Engineer
CRCT	Commander Royal Corps of Transport
CRE	Central Reconnaissance Establishment
	Commander Royal Engineers

CREA	Chief Radio Electrical Artificer
CREL	Chief Radio Electrician
CREME	Commander Royal Electrical & Mechanical Engineers
CREMN	Chief Radio Electrical Mechanician
CRH	Calibre-Radius Head
CRO	Chief Recruiting Officer
	Civilian Repair Organisation
CRP	Control and Reporting Post
CRS(S)	Chief Radio Supervisor (Special)
(W)	(Warfare)
CRT	Canadian Railway Troops
CRU	Civilian Repair Unit
	Corps Reinforcement Unit
CRVC	Cambridgeshire Rifle Volunteer Corps
CRW	Counter-Revolutionary Warfare
CS	Capital Ship [Bomb]
	Continuous Service
	Coppersmith
	Cruiser, Scout
	Cruiser Squadron
CSBA	Chief Sick Berth Attendant
CSBS	Course Setting Bombsight
CSC	Commissariat Staff Corps
	Conspicuous Service Cross
CSCB	Civil Service Cadet Battalion
CSDIC	Combined Services Detailed Interrogation Centre
CSE	Combined Services Entertainment
CSEF	Canadian Siberian Expeditionary Force
CSEU	Combined Services Entertainment Unit
CSFC	Church of Scotland & Free Churches
C/Sgt	Colour Sergeant
CSIGO	Chief Signals Officer
CSLMR	Chief Sailmaker
CSM	Committee of Special Means
	Company Sergeant-Major
CSMI	Company Sergeant-Major Instructor
CSNM	Chief Superintendent of Naval Meteorology
CSO	Chief Signal Officer
	Chief Staff Officer
CSRD	Chief Superintendent Research Department
CSRV	Civil Service Rifle Volunteers
CSSAD	Committee for the Scientific Study of Air Defence
CSSAO	Committee for the Scientific Study of Air Offence
CSTC	Combined Strategic Targets Committee
CSWA	Captain Surface Weapons Acceptance
CSWS	Crew Served Weapon Sight

27

CT	Communication Trench
CTC	Cape Town Cavalry
	Combined Training Centre
	Commando Training Centre
	Commissariat & Transport Corps
CTCRM	Commando Training Centre Royal Marines
CTF	Combined Task Force
	Commander, Task Force
CTG	Combined Task Group
	Commander, Task Group
CTI	Competent To Instruct
CTL	Constructive Total Loss
CT O	Catering Officer
CTS	Composite Training School
CTU	Commander, Task Unit
CU	Conversion Unit
CUOTC	Cambridge University Officer Training Corps
CUR	Cambridge University Rifles
CV	Command Vehicle
CVBC	Cape Volunteer Bearer Corps
CVL	Calcutta Volunteer Lancers
CVR(T)	Combat Vehicle, Reconnaissance (Tracked)
CVR(W)	Combat Vehicle, Reconnaissance (Wheeled)
CW	Chemical Warfare
	Commander's Office Writer
	Commission & Warrant
CWAC	Canadian Women's Army Corps
CWGC	Commonwealth War Graves Commission
CWO	Canadian War Office
	Command Works Office
	Commissioned Officer from Warrant Rank
CWRENAF	Chief Wren Air Fitter
CWRENCINE	Chief Wren Cinema Operator
CWRENCK	Chief Wren Cook
CWRENDHYG	Chief Wren Dental Hygienist
CWRENDSA	Chief Wren Dental Surgery Assistant
CWRENEDUC	Chief Wren Education Assistant
CWRENMET	Chief Wren Meteorological Observer
CWRENPHOT	Chief Wren Photographer
CWRENQA	Chief Wren Quarters Assistant
CWREN(R)	Chief Wren (Radar)
CWRENREG	Chief Wren Regulating
CWRENREL	Chief Wren Radio Electrician
CWRENRS(M)	Chief Wren Radio Supervisor (Morse)
CWRENSA	Chief Wren Stores Accountant
CWRENS(C)	Chief Wren Stores Assistant (Clothes)

(V)	(Victualling)
CWRENSTD	Chief Wren Steward
CWRENTEL	Chief Wren Telephonist
CWRENTSA	Chief Wren Training Support Assistant
CWRENWA	Chief Wren Weapon Analyst
CWRENWTR(G)	Chief Wren Writer (General)
(P)	(Pay)
CWRENWW	Chief Wren Welfare Worker
CWWF	Churches Committee for Work among Women serving with HM Forces
CY	Communication Yeoman
CYC	Canterbury Yeomanry Cavalry
CYDEF	Cyrenaica Defence Force
CYR	Carleton & York Regiment
D	Deserted
	Destroyer
	Discharged
	Diver
	Dragoons
	Driver
DA	Defence Adviser
	Delayed Action
	Dispensing Allowance
DAAG	Deputy Assistant Adjutant-General
DAA & QMG	Deputy Assistant Adjutant & Quartermaster General
DAC	Divisional Ammunition Column
DACG	Deputy Assistant Commissary General
DACOS	Deputy Assistant Chief of Staff
DACR	Director of Airfields & Carrier Requirements
DADGMS	Deputy Assistant Director General of Medical Services
DADIWT	Deputy Assistant Director of Inland Water Transport
DADME	Deputy Assistant Director of Mechanical Engineering
DADMS	Deputy Assistant Director of Medical Services
DADOS	Deputy Assistant Director of Ordnance Services
DADPR	Deputy Assistant Director of Public Relations
DADPTC	Defence Automatic Data Processing Training Centre
DADR	Deputy Assistant Director of Remounts
DADRT	Deputy Assistant Director of Railway Transport
DADS & T	Deputy Assistant Director of Supplies & Transport
DADVRS	Deputy Assistant Director of Veterinary & Remount Services
DADVS	Deputy Assistant Director of Veterinary Services
DAE	Director of Aircraft Equipment
DAF	Desert Air Force
DAG	Deputy Adjutant-General

29

DAGRA	Deputy Adjutant-General Royal Artillery
DAJAG	Deputy Assistant Judge Advocate General
DALS	Director of Army Legal Services
DAM	Director of Air Material
DAMF	Director of Air Ministry Factories
DAMR	Director of Aircraft Maintenance & Repair
DANS	Director of Army Nursing Services
DAOC	Deputy Air Officer Commanding
DAOC-in-C	Deputy Air Officer Commanding-in-Chief
DAOT	Director of Air Organisation & Training
DAP	Director of Aeroplane Production
	Director of Ammunition Production
DAPM	Deputy Assistant Provost Marshal
DAPS	Director of Army Postal Services
DAQMG	Deputy Assistant Quartermaster-General
DAS	Director of Armament Supply
	Doyle's Australian Scouts
DASD	Director Anti-Submarine Division
	Director of Army Staff Duties
DASH	Destroyer Anti-Submarine Helicopter
	Drone Anti-Submarine Helicopter
DASWE	Director, Admiralty Surface Weapons Establishment
DATS	Director, Auxiliary Territorial Service
DAUWE	Director, Admiralty Underwater Weapons Establishment
DAW	Director of Naval Air Warfare
DAWS	Director of Army Welfare Services
DAWT	Director of Air Warfare & Training
DB	Dental Branch
	Double Bottoms
DBC	Director of Barrack Construction
DBO	Dawn Battle Order
	District Barrack Officer
DB Ops	Director of Bomber Operations
DC	Depth Charge
DCAM	Director of Craft & Amphibious Material
DCAS	Deputy Chief of Air Staff
DCC	Damage Control Centre
DCD	Director of Compass Department
DCDS	Deputy Chief of Defence Staff
DCGS	Deputy Chief of the General Staff
DCHQ	Damage Control Headquarters
DCI	Defence Council Instruction
DCIGS	Deputy Chief of the Imperial General Staff
DCLI	Duke of Cornwall's Light Infantry
DCM	Distinguished Conduct Medal
	District Court Martial

DCNEO	Deputy Chief Naval Engineering Officer
DCNI	Department of the Chief of Naval Information
DCNS	Deputy Chief of the Naval Staff
DCO	Director of Combined Operations
	Duke of Cambridge's Own
	Duke/Duchess of Connaught's Own
DCOS	Deputy Chief(s) of Staff
DC(P)	Deputy Controller (Polaris)
DCRCH	Duke of Connaught's Royal Canadian Hussars
DCRE	Deputy Commander Royal Engineers
DCSO	Deputy Chief Signal Officer
DCT	Depth Charge Thrower
	Director Control Tower
DCU	Disbandment Control Unit
DD	Discharged Dead
	Dockyard Department
	Duplex Drive
D & D	Devonshire & Dorset Regiment
DDANS	Deputy Director of Army Nursing Services
DDATS	Deputy Director, Auxiliary Territorial Service
DDB Ops	Deputy Director of Bomber Operations
DDDS	Deputy Director of Dental Services
DDGMR	Deputy Director-General of Military Railways
DDGT	Deputy Director-General of Transportation
DDHG	Deputy Director Home Guard
DDHO	Deputy Director of Home Operations
DDI	Deputy Director of Intelligence
DDIWT	Deputy Director of Inland Water Transport
DDME	Deputy Director of Mechanical Engineering
DDMI	Deputy Director of Military Intelligence
DDMO & I	Deputy Director of Military Operations & Intelligence
DDMS	Deputy Director of Medical Services
DDMT	Deputy Director of Military Training
DDNI	Deputy Director of Naval Intelligence
DDO	Deputy Director of Organisation
DDOATS	Deputy Director of Organisation, Auxiliary Territorial Service
DDOD	Deputy Director Operations Division
DDOI	Deputy Director of Operations & Intelligence
DDOS	Deputy Director of Ordnance Services
DDS	Director of Dental Services
DDSD	Deputy Director of Staff Duties
DDST	Deputy Director of Supplies & Transport
DDVRS	Deputy Director Veterinary Remount Service
DDVS	Deputy Director of Veterinary Services
DDWP	Deputy Directorate Weapons Polaris

DEA	Davis Escape Apparatus
DED	Director of Education Department
def	defence
DEFREP	Defence Readiness Position
DEG	Destroyer Escort, Guided Missile
DEL	Defence Electric Light
DEMS	Defensively Equipped Merchant Ship
DE(N)	Director of Engineering (Naval)
DEOS	Director of Equipment & Ordnance Stores
DEOVR	Duke of Edinburgh's Own Volunteer Rifles
DERR	Duke of Edinburgh's Royal Regiment
Det	Detached
	Detachment
Detmt	Detachment
Detn	Detention
DEW	Distant Early Warning
DF	Defence Fellow
	Defensive Fire
	Destroyer Flotilla
	[Royal] Dublin Fusiliers
D/F	Direction Finding
DFLS	Day Fighter Leaders School
DFA	Diamonds Fields Artillery
DFC	Distinguished Flying Cross
DF/GA	Day Fighter/Ground Attack
DFM	Director of Fleet Maintenance
	Distinguished Flying Medal
DFSD	Directorate of Fleet Supply Duties
DFT	Director of Flying Training
DFW	Director of Fortifications & Works
DG	Degaussing
	District Guard
	Dragoon Guards
Dg	Diving
DGAMS	Director-General Army Medical Services
DGA(N)	Director-General Aircraft (Naval)
DGAR	Director-General of Army Requirements
DGAVS	Director-General of the Army Veterinary Service
DGD	Director of Ground Defence
	Director Gunnery Division
DGE	Director-General of Equipment
DGFV	Director-General of Fighting Vehicles
DGHG	Director-General Home Guard
DGM	Destroyer, Guided Missile
DGMR	Director-General of Military Railways
DGMS	Director-General of Medical Services

DGMT	Director-General of Military Training
DGMW	Director-General of Military Works
DGNMT	Director-General Naval Manpower & Training
DGNPD	Director-General of Naval Development & Production
DGO	Director-General of Organization
DGPS(N)	Director-General Personal Services (Naval)
DGST	Director General Supply & Transport
DGT	Director-General of Training
	Director-General of Transportation
DGTA	Director-General of the Territorial Army
DGTF	Director-General of the Territorial Force
DGV	Degaussing Vessel
DGW	Director-General of Weapons
DH	Deccan Horse
	De Havilland
	Dental Hygienist
	Director of Hygiene
DHIY	Denbighshire Hussars Imperial Yeomanry
DHO	Director of Home Operations
DHQ	District Headquarters
	Divisional Headquarters
DI	Daily Inspection
	Director of Infantry
	Drill Instructor
DID	Detail Issue Depot
	Director of the Intelligence Division
DIS	Daily Issue Store
	Defence Intelligence Staff
Dist	District
Div	Division
DIVYEO	Diving Yeoman
DIWT	Director of Inland Water Transport
DIY	Derbyshire Imperial Yeomanry
DJAG	Deputy Judge Advocate General
DL	Defence Light
	Director Layer
	Drill Leader
DLCO	Deck Landing Control Officer
DLI	Durham Light Infantry
DLO	Duke of Lancaster's Own
DLOY	Duke of Lancaster's Own Yeomanry
DLPS	Deck Landing Projector Sight
DLS	Defence Light Section
	Director of Legal Services
DLT	Deck Landing-Training
DLT/P	Deck Landing Training/Practice

DM	Dental Mechanic
	Devon Militia
	Director of Mobilization
	Director of Music
	Driver Mechanic
D/Maj	Drum-Major
DME	Director of Mechanical Engineering
DMGO	Divisional Machine Gun Officer
DMI	Director of Military Intelligence
DMM	Director of Mechanical Maintenance
DMO	Director of Military Operations
DMO & I	Director of Military Operations and Intelligence
DMOS(N)	Director of Meteorological & Oceanographical Services (Naval)
DMPD	Director of Dockyard Manpower & Productivity
DMR	Director of Medical Research
DMR(N)	Director of Materials Research (Naval)
DMS	Difference of Messing Subscription
	Direct Moulded Sole
	Director of Medical Services
DMSC	Defence Material Standardization Committee
DMS(N)	Director of Marine Services (Naval)
DMT	Director of Military Training
Dn	Dragoon
D/N	Day & Night
DNA	Director of Navy Accounts
DNAP	Directorate of Naval Administrative Planning
DNAW	Directorate of Naval Air Warfare
DNC	Director of Naval Construction
DND	Department of National Defence [Canada]
	Director of Navigation & Direction
DNDS	Director of Naval Dental Services
DNE	Director of Naval Equipment
DNES	Director of Naval Education Service
DNET	Director of Naval Engineering Training
DNFCT	Director of Naval Foreign & Commonwealth Training
DNFPS	Director, Naval Future Policy Staff
DNGW	Director of Naval Guided Weapons
DNI	Director of Naval Intelligence
DNM	Director of Naval Manning
DNMO	Director of Naval Management & Organization
DNMP	Director of Naval Manpower Planning
DNMR	Director of Naval Manpower Requirements
	Director of Naval Manpower Resources
DNMS	Director of Naval Medical Services
DNMSP	Director of Naval Manpower Structure Planning

DNMT	Director of Naval Manning & Training
DNO	Director of Naval Operations
	Director of Naval Ordnance
DNOA	Director of Naval Officer Appointments
DNOR	Director of Naval Operational Requirements
DNOS	Director of Naval Operational Studies
DNOT	Director of Naval Operations & Trade
DNPTS	Director of Naval Physical Training & Sport
DNR	Director of Naval Recruiting
DNS	Director of Naval Signals
DNSC	Director of Naval Service Conditions
DNSY	Director of Naval Security
DNT	Director of Naval Training
DNTO	Divisional Naval Transport Officer
DNW	Director of Naval Warfare
DNWC	Director of Naval Weapons Contracts
DNWS	Director, Naval Weather Service
DO	District Officer
DOA	Director of Officer Appointments
DOAE	Defence Operational Analysis Establishment
DOC	District Officer Commanding
DOD	Director, Operations Division
DODAR	Director of Drafting and Records
DOF	Director of Ordnance Factories
D of A	Director of Artillery
D of C	Director of Contracts
D of D	Director of Dockyards
D of I	Director of Intelligence
D of M	Director of Manning
D of O	Director of Organization
D of PD	Director of Plans Division
D of Q	Director of Quartering
D of S	Director of Stores
D of V	Director of Victualling
DOO	Directing Ordnance Officer
DORA	Defence of the Realm Act
DORS	Defence Operational Requirements
DOS	Director of Ordnance Services
DOT	Director of Operational Training
DOTM	Director of Naval Ordnances, Torpedoes & Mines
DP	Delivery Point
	Detained Pay
	Director of Postings
	Distribution Point
	Drill Purposes
	Dual Purpose

35

DPACCS	Displaced Person Assembly Centre Camp Staffs
DPC	Defence Planning Committee
DPCC	Director of Postal & Courier Communications
DPF	Depression Position Finder
DPM	Deputy Provost Marshal
	Disruptive Pattern Material
DPR	Director of Public Relations
DPRC	Defence Policy & Requirements Committee
DPRORM	Drafting, Pay & Records Office, Royal Marines
DPS	Defence Policy Staff
	Director of Personal Services
DQ	Detention Quarters
DQMG	Deputy Quartermaster-General
DR	Dead Reckoning
	Despatch Rider
	Director of Remounts
Dr	Driver
	Drummer
DRA	Director Royal Artillery
DRAC	Director Royal Armoured Corps
Dragns	Dragoons
DRC	Defence Requirements Committee
DRE	Director of Radio Equipment
DRF	Depression Range Finder
DRLS	Despatch Rider Letter Service
DRO	Daily Routine Orders
	Director of Recruiting & Organization
	Divisional Records Office
	Divisional Routine Orders
DRORM	Drafting & Records Office, Royal Marines
DRS	Director of Repair & Service
DRT	Director of Railway Transport
DS	Directing Staff
	Director of Signals
	Discarding Sabot
DSA	Dental Surgery Assistant
DSASO	Deputy Senior Air Staff Officer
DSB	Defence Signal Board
	Duty Steam Boat
DSC	Distinguished Service Cross
DSD	Director of Signals Division
	Director of Staff Duties
DSEA	Davis Submerged Escape Apparatus
D/Sgt	Drill Sergeant
DSM	Distinguished Service Medal
	Divisional Sergeant-Major

DSO	Distinguished Service Order
DSOAG	Deputy Senior Officer Assault Group
DSQ	Director of Supplies & Quartering
	Discharged to Sick Quarters
DSRV	Deep-Submergence Rescue Vessel
DSST	Director of Supply & Secretariat Training
DST	Director of Sea Transport
	Director of Supplies & Transport
DS/T	Discarding Sabot/Training
DSTO	District Supply & Transport Officer
DSVY	Director of Survey
DSWP	Director of Surface Weapons Projects
DT	Director of Transport
DTASW	Director, Torpedo, Anti-Submarine & Mine Warfare
DTD	Department of Tank Design
	Director of Technical Development
DTGW	Director of Guided Weapons Trials
DTL	Deep Trench Latrine
DTM	Director of Transport & Movements
DTN	Defence Telecommunications Network
DTP	Driver Training Platoon
DTSD	Director of Tactical & Staff Duties Division
	Director of Training & Staff Duties
DTT	Director of Technical Training
DUKW	D = 1942 / U = utility / K = all-wheel drive / W = twin rear wheel axles
DUSW	Director of Undersea Warfare
DUW	Director of Underwater Weapons
DVO	Divisional Veterinary Officer
DVR	Van Riebeeck Decoration
Dvr	Driver
DVS	Director of Veterinary Services
DW	Director of Works
	Duke of Wellington's Regiment
DWAAF	Director of Women's Auxiliary Air Force
DWES	Director of Weapons Equipment, Surface
DWEU	Director of Weapons Equipment, Underwater
DWI	Directional Wireless Installation
DWP	Director of Weapons Production
DWR	Duke of Wellington's Regiment
DWRAF	Director of the Women's Royal Air Force
DWRDS	Director, Weapons Research & Development, Surface
DWRDU	Director, Weapons Research & Development, Underwater
DWRP	Director of Weapons Resources & Programmes
DWSC	Director of Welfare & Service Conditions
DWT	Deck-Watch Time

DY	Derbyshire Yeomanry
	Dockyard
DYO	Duke of York's Own
DYS	Duke of York's Royal Military School
DZ	Dropping Zone
E	Enfield
	Engineering
	European
EA	Electrical Artificer
	Engineer Admiral
	Entertaining Allowance
E/A	Enemy Aircraft
EAA	East African Artillery
EA(A)1	Electrical Artificer Air 1st Class
2	2nd class
3	3rd class
EA(A)APP	Electrical Artificer (Air) Apprentice
EAAC	East African Armoured Corps
EAAEC	East African Army Educational Corps
EAAMC	East African Army Medical Corps
EAAOC	East African Army Ordnance Corps
EAB	Enemy Activities Branch
EAEME	East African Electrical & Mechanical Engineers
EAMLS	East African Military Labour Service
EAPC	East African Pioneer Corps
EARC	East African Reconnaissance Corps
EARS	East African Reconnaissance Squadron
EASC	East African Service Corps
EASTOMP	Eastern Ocean Meeting Point
EATS	Empire Air Training Scheme
EAVC	Edinburgh Artillery Volunteer Corps
EAWP	Eastern Atlantic War Plan
EBE	Experimental Bridging Establishment
EBSRVR	East Bengal State Railway Volunteer Rifles
EC	Eastern Command
	Engineer Captain
	Exercise Commander
ECCM	Electronic Counter-Counter-Measures
ECIY	Earl of Chester's Imperial Yeomanry
ECM	Electronic Counter-Measures
ECO	Emergency Commissioned Officer
ECP	Equipment Collecting Point
ECR	Enemy Contact Report
ECr	Engineer Commander
ECYC	Earl of Chester's Yeomanry Cavalry

ED	Education Department
	Efficiency Decoration
EDC	European Defence Community
EDE	Experimental Demolition Establishment
EDR	Electrical Distance Recorder
EE	Electrical Engineers
EEF	Egyptian Expeditionary Force
EF	Expeditionary Force
EFA	[Category] E Flying Accident
EFB	Experimental Fighting Biplane
EFC	Escort Force Commander
	Expeditionary Force Canteens
EFI	Expeditionary Force Institutes
EFTS	Elementary Flying Training School
EG	Experimental Assistant, Gunnery
EGM	Empire Gallantry Medal
EGMR	East Griqualand Mounted Rifles
EGS	Elementary Gliding School
EHG	Edinburgh Home Guard
EI	Enemy Intelligence
EIC	East India Company
EICS	East India Company's Service
E-in-C	Engineer-in-Chief
E-in-CD	Engineer-in-Chief's Department
EKVF	East Kent Volunteer Fencibles
EL	Electrician
	Engineer Lieutenant
E LAN R	East Lancashire Regiment
E L Cr	Engineer Lieutenant-Commander
ELI	European Light Infantry
ELINT	Electronic Intelligence
ELMN (A)1	Electrical Mechanician (Air) 1st Class
2	2nd Class
3	3rd Class
ELMN(AW)1	Electrical Mechanician (Air Weapon) 1st Class
2	2nd Class
3	3rd Class
ELYC	East Lothian Yeomanry Cavalry
EM	Efficiency Medal
	Enlisted Man
EM(A)1	Electrical Mechanic (Air) 1st Class
2	2nd Class
EM(AW)1	Electrical Mechanic (Air Weapon) 1st Class
2	2nd Class
EMAE	Electrical & Mechanical Assistant Engineer
EME	Electrical & Mechanical Engineer

EMMGB	Eaton's Motor Machine Gun Battery
EMO	Embarkation Medical Officer
ENCA	European Naval Communications Agency
ENCP	European Naval Communications Plan
Eng	Engineer
Engr	Engineer
En L	Engineer Lieutenant
En L Cr	Engineer Lieutenant-Commander
ENSA	Entertainments National Service Association
En SL	Engineer Sub-Lieutenant
EO	Education Officer
	Engineer Officer
EOD	Explosive Ordnance Disposal
EP	Egyptian Pattern
	Extension Pay
EPR	Eastern Pakistan Rifles
EPS	Executive Planning Section
	Exercise Planning Staff
ER	Equipment Repairer
ERA	Engine Room Artificer
ERD	Army Emergency Reserve Decoration
ERE	Extra-Regimentally Employed
E & RFTS	Elementary & Reserve Flying Training School
ERY	East Riding Yeomanry
ERYIY	East Riding of Yorkshire Imperial Yeomanry
ES	Eagle Squadron
	Enginesmith
E/S	Electrode Signalling
ESBA	Eastern Sovereign Base Area
ESD	Equipment Supply Depot
ESM	East Surrey Militia
	Electronic Support Measures
ESO	Embarkation Staff Officer
Estt	Establishment
ET	Educational Test
ETA	Estimated Time of Arrival
ETD	Estimated Time of Departure
ETE	Experimental Tunnelling Establishment
ETPS	Empire Test Pilots School
ETR	Estimated Time of Return
ETW	Equipment Trials Wing
EV	Engineer Volunteers
EVA	Essex Volunteer Artillery
EVC	Engineer Volunteer Corps
EVRC	Eton Volunteer Rifle Corps
EVT	Education & Vocational Training

40

EW	Early Warning
	Electronic Warfare
	Engineer's Writer
EWAD	Early Warning Air Defence
EWD	Economic Warfare Division
EWMB	Enemy War Materials Branch
EWR	Early Warning Radar
EY	East Yorkshire [Militia]
	Essex Yeomanry
EYR	East Yorkshire Regiment
F	Fighter
	Fitter
	Fleet
	Flying
FA	Field Allowance
	Field Artillery
FAA	Fleet Air Arm
FAASTU	Fleet Air Arm Service Trials Unit
FAC	Forward Air Controller
FACE	Field Artillery Computer Equipment
FAL	Fusil Automatique Legere
FAM	Fast Aerial Mine
F Amb	Field Ambulance
FAMO	Forward Air Maintenance Organization
FANY	First Aid Nursing Yeomanry
FANYS	First Aid Nursing Yeomanry Service
FAO	Fleet Accountant Officer
FARELF	Far East Land Forces
FAT	Field Artillery Tractor
FATC	Field Artillery Training Centre
FAU	Friends Ambulance Unit
FAV	Forfar Artillery Volunteers
FAVO	Fleet Aviation Officer
FAW	Fighter, All Weather
FB	Fighter-Bomber
	Flying Boat
FBE	Folding Boat Equipment
FBRD	Flying Boat Repair Depot
F/Bt	Flying Boat
FC	Ferry Command
	Fighter Command
	Fire Control Armourer
	Fire Commander
	Forage Corps
FCA	Fleet Chief Armourer

41

FCAA	Fleet Chief Aircraft Artificer
FCACMN .	Fleet Chief Aircrewman
FCAF	Fleet Chief Air Fitter
FACMN	Fleet Chief Aircraft Mechanician
FCCA	Fleet Chief Caterer
FCCEA	Fleet Chief Control Electrical Artificer
FCCEL	Fleet Chief Control Electrician
FCCEMN	Fleet Chief Electrical Mechanician
FCCK	Fleet Chief Cook
FCCY	Fleet Chief Communication Yeoman
FCEA	Fleet Chief Electrical Artificer
FCEL(A)	Fleet Chief Electrician (Air)
FCEL(AW)	Fleet Chief Electrician (Air Weapon)
FCELMN(A)	Fleet Chief Electrical Mechanician (Air)
FCELMN(AW)	Fleet Chief Electrical Mechanician (Air Weapon)
FCM	Farrier Corporal-Major
FCMA	Field Cashier Military Accounts
	Fleet Chief Medical Assistant
FCMEA	Fleet Chief Marine Engineering Artificer
FCMEM	Fleet Chief Marine Engineering Mechanic
FCMT	Fleet Chief Medical Technician
FCO	Fleet Communications Officer
	Flying Control Officer
F Co	Field Company
FCOEA	Fleet Chief Ordnance Electrical Artificer
FCOEL	Fleet Chief Ordnance Electrician
FCOEMN	Fleet Chief Ordnance Electrical Mechanician
FCP	Ferry Command Police
FCPO	Fleet Chief Petty Officer
FCPT	Fleet Chief Physical Trainer
FCREA	Fleet Chief Radio Electrical Artificer
FCREL(A)	Fleet Chief Radio Electrician (Air)
FCREMN	Fleet Chief Radio Electrical Mechanician
FCRS(S)	Fleet Chief Radio Supervisor (Special)
FCRS(W)	Fleet Chief Radio Supervisor (Warfare)
FCS	Fighter Catapult Ship
	Fire Control System
FCSA	Fleet Chief Stores Accountant
FCSTD	Fleet Chief Steward
FCTB	Featherston Camp Trumpet Band
FCWRENAF	Fleet Chief Wren Air Fitter
FCWRENCINE	Fleet Chief Wren Cinema Operator
FCWRENCK	Fleet Chief Wren Cook
FCWRENDHYG	Fleet Chief Wren Dental Hygienist
FCWRENDSA	Fleet Chief Wren Dental Surgery Assistant
FCWRENEDUC	Fleet Chief Wren Education Assistant

FCWRENMET	Fleet Chief Wren Meteorological Observer
FCWRENPHOT	Fleet Chief Wren Photographer
FCWRENQA	Fleet Chief Wren Quarters Assistant
FCWREN(R)	Fleet Chief Wren (Radar)
FCWRENREG	Fleet Chief Wren Regulating
FCWRENREL	Fleet Chief Wren Radio Electrician
FCWRENRS(M)	Fleet Chief Wren Radio Supervisor (Morse)
FCWRENSA	Fleet Chief Wren Stores Accountant
FCWRENSTD	Fleet Chief Wren Steward
FCWRENTEL	Fleet Chief Wren Telephonist
FCWRENTSA	Fleet Chief Wren Training Support Assistant
FCWRENWA	Fleet Chief Wren Weapon Analyst
FCWRENWTR (G)	Fleet Chief Wren Writer (General)
FCWRENWTR (P)	Fleet Chief Wren Writer (Pay)
FCWRENWW	Fleet Chief Wren Welfare Worker
FD	Fleet Duties
Fd	Field
FDO	Fighter Direction Officer
	Flight Deck Officer
FDS	Fleet Dental Surgeon
	Forward Delivery Squadron
FDT	Fighter Direction Tender
FDVS	Field Depot Veterinary Stores
FE	Farman Experimental
	First Entry
	Fit for Service Everywhere
F/E	Flight Engineer
FEAF	Far East Air Force
FEBA	Forward Edge of the Battle Area
FECB	Far East Combined Bureau
FELF	Far East Land Forces
FEO	Fleet Engineer Officer
FF	Field Force
	Firefighter
	Frontier Force
FFI	Free from Infection
F & FIY	Fife & Forfar Imperial Yeomanry
FFR	Fitted for Radio
	Frontier Force Rifles
FFW	Fitted for Wireless
F & FY	Fife & Forfar Yeomanry
FFY/SH	Fife & Forfar Yeomanry/Scottish Horse
FG	Field Gun
	Fine Grain

43

F/GA	Fighter/Ground Attack
FGCM	Field General Court-Martial
FGH	Fort Garry Horse
FGO	Fleet Gunnery Officer
Fg Off	Flying Officer
FGRI	Fixed Ground Radio Installations
FGS	Fancy Goods Store
FH	Fane's Horse
	Field Hospital
	Field Howitzer
FID	Field Intelligence Department
FIDO	Fog, Intensive, Dispersal of
	Fog Investigation & Dispersal Operation
F Imp	Field Imprisonment
FINCO	Field Intelligence Non-Commissioned Officer
FIO	Field Intelligence Officer
	Fleet Instructor Officer
FIS	Flying Instrument School
FIU	Fighter Interception Unit
F & K RGA	Fife & Kincardine Royal Garrison Artillery
FL	Flight Lieutenant
F/L	Flintlock
FLAK	Flieger Abwehr Kanone
Fld Amb	Field Ambulance
FLEWEACEN	Fleet Weather Centre
FLEX	Fleet Exercise
FLH	Fife Light Horse
FLHV	Fife Light Horse Volunteers
FLO	Fleet Electrical Officer
Fl/O	Flying Officer
Fl Offr	Flying Officer
FLS	Fighter Leader School
Flt	Flight
F/Lt	Flight Lieutenant
Flt Lieut	Flight Lieutenant
FLYCO	Commander Flying
	Flying Control
FM	Field Marshal
FMA	Forward Maintenance Area
FMAA	Fleet Master-at-Arms
FMC	Forces Motoring Club
FMC-in-C	Field Marshal Commanding-in-Chief
FMEO	Fleet Marine Engineering Officer
FMETO	Fleet Meteorological Officer
FMO	Fleet Medical Officer
	Full Marching Order

FMR	Fife Mounted Rifles
	Frontier Mounted Rifles
	Les Fusiliers Mont Royal
FMVEME	Federation of Malaya Volunteer Electrical & Mechanical Engineers
FMSVR	Federated Malay Straits Volunteer Reserve
FMVRC	Federation of Malaya Volunteer Reconnaissance Corps
FN	Fabrique National d'Armes de Guerre
FNSF	Fast Night Striking Force
FO	Field Officer
	Flag Officer
F/O	Flying Officer
FOB	Forward Observer, Bombardment
	Forward Operating Base
FOBAA	Flag Officer British Assault Area
FOCAS	Flag Officer, Carriers & Amphibious Ships
FOCNAS	Flag Officer Commanding North Atlantic Station
FOCRIN	Flag Officer Commanding Royal Indian Navy
FOCT	Flag Officer, Carrier Training
FOD	Foreign Object Damage
FOF 1	Flag Officer, First Flotilla
2	Second Flotilla
FOIC	Flag Officer in Charge
FONAC	Flag Officer Naval Air Command
FONAS	Flag Officer Naval Air Stations
FONF	Flag Officer Newfoundland
FOO	Fleet Operations Officer
	Forward Observation Officer
FORY	Flag Officer Royal Yachts
FOSM	Flag Officer Submarines
FOST	Flag Officer Sea Training
FOW	Formation Ordnance Workshop
FP	Field Punishment
fp	full pay
FPB	Fast Patrol Boat
FPO	Field Post Office
FPP	Ferry Pilots School
FPU	Film Production Unit
FQMS	Farrier Quartermaster-Sergeant
FR	Fighter Reconnaissance
	Forest Rangers
FRADU	Fleet Requirements & Aircraft Direction Unit
FRATU	Fleet Requirements & Aircraft Training Unit
FRD	Field Remount Depot
FRMO	Fleet Royal Marines Officer
FRO	Fleet Recreations Officer

FRR	[Royal Irish] Fusiliers Reserve Regiment
FRU	Fleet Requirements Unit
FS	Fairbairn-Sykes
	Field Security
	Field Service
	Fleet Surgeon
	Flying Scholarship
FSC	Field Survey Company
F/Sgt	Flight Sergeant
FSL	Foreign Service Leave
FSM	Field Service Manual
FSMO	Field Service Marching Order
FSO	Field Security Officer
	Fleet Supply Officer
FSP	Field Security Personnel
	Field Security Police
FSPB	Field Service Pocket Book
FSR	Field Service Regulations
	First Surrey Rifles
	Fleet Spotter Reconnaissance
FSYO	Field Security Officer
FT	Fitter & Turner
	Foretop
FTB	Fast Torpedo Boat
	Fleet Torpedo Bomber
FTC	Flying Training Command
FTO	Fleet Torpedo Officer
FTR	Failed to Return
Ftr	Fighter
FTS	Flying Training School
FTU	Ferry Training Unit
FUP	Forming-Up Place
Fus	Fusilier
FV	Fighting Vehicle
FVDE	Fighting Vehicles Design Establishment
FVRDE	Fighting Vehicle Research & Development Establishment
FVS	Fighting Vehicle System
FWEO	Fleet Weapons Engineering Officer
FWO	Fleet Wireless Officer
FWW	First World War
FX	Forecastle
G	Glider
	Grog
	Guards
	Gunnery

GA	Garrison Adjutant
	Garrison Artillery
	Gunlayer Armourer
GarmO	Group Armaments Officer
GASC	Gurkha Army Service Corps
GATCO	Group Air Traffic Control Officer
GB	Gunboat
GBG	Governor's Bodyguard
GC	Garrison Company
	Gentleman Cadet
	Good Conduct
	Gun Carriage
	Gun Captain
G/C	Group Captain
GCA	Ground Control Apparatus
	Ground Controlled Approach
G/Capt	Group Captain
GCatO	Group Catering Officer
GCB	Good Conduct Badge
GCCS	Government Code & Cypher School
GCI	Ground Controlled Interception
GCL	Ground Control Landing
GCM	General Court-Martial
GCO	Governor's Commissioned Officer
	Gun Control Officer
GCR	Gold Coast Regiment
GCT	Gun Control Tower
GCTF	Gold Coast Territorial Force
GD	General Duty
	Gunnery Division
Gd	Guard
GDF	Gibraltar Defence Force
GD(G)	General Duties (Ground)
GDP	General Defence Plan
	Gun Defence Position
Gds	Guards
Gdsm	Guardsman
GDX	Gun Direction Exercise
GE	Garrison Engineer
GEdO	Group Education Officer
GEM	Ground-Effect Machine
Gen	General
Genl	General
GESO	Group Equipment Staff Officer
GF	Grand Fleet
	Gunnery Flight

47

GFBI	Grand Fleet Battle Instructions
GFBO	Grand Fleet Battle Orders
GG	Grenadier Guards
	Ground Gunner
GGBG	Governor-General's Bodyguard
GGC	Gun Group Commander
GGO	Governor-General's Order
GHP	Greenwich Hospital Pension
GHQ	General Headquarters
GI	Gunnery Instructor
GIO	Group Intelligence Officer
GIP	Garden Island Prison
GIY	Glamorgan Imperial Yeomanry
GL	General List
	Gunlayer
	Gunnery Lieutenant
GLI	Gurkha Light Infantry
GLO	Ground Liaison Officer
GLW	Gunnery Lieutenant's Writer
GM	Grog Money
	Guided Missile
	Gunner's Mate
GMCM	Guided Missile Counter-Measure
GMetO	Group Meteorological Officer
GMGB	Guards Machine Gun Battalion
GMGR	Guards Machine Gun Regiment
GMP	Garrison Military Police
	Gurkha Military Police
GNavO	Group Navigation Officer
Gnr	Gunner
GNS	General Naval Staff
GNT	General Naval Training
GO	Garrison Orders
	Gas Operated
	General Officer
	General Order
	Group Officer
	Gunnery Officer
	Gurkha Officer
GOC	General Officer Commanding
GOCC	General Order of the Commander-in-Chief
GOC-in-C	General Officer Commanding-in-Chief
GOI	Group Operations Instruction
GOO	Group Operations Order
GOP	General Operations Plot
GOR	Gun Operations Room

GOTU	Glider Operational Training Unit
GOW	Gunnery Officer's Writer
GP	General Purpose [Bomb]
Gp	Group
Gp Capt	Group Captain
GPD	General Police Duties
GPM	Gunnery Prize Money
GPMG	General Purpose Machine Gun
GPO	Gun Position Officer
GPOA	Gun Position Officer's Assistant
Gp Offr	Group Officer
GPR	Glider Pilot Regiment
GPT	General Purpose Transport
GQMS	Garrison Quartermaster-Sergeant
GR	Gambia Regiment
	General Reconnaissance
	Gloucestershire Regiment
	Gurkha Rifles
Gr	Group
	Gunner
Gr Capt	Group Captain
GRegO	Group Regiment Officer
GREF	General Reserve Engineer Force
GRO	General Routine Order
Grp Capt	Group Captain
GRRC	Gurkha Rifles Regimental Centre
GRS	General Reconnaissance School
Gr(T)	Gunner (Torpedo)
GS	General Service
	General Staff
	Gliding School
GSC	General Service Corps
GSigsO	Group Signals Officer
GSL	General Service Launch
GSM	Garrison Sergeant-Major
GSO 1	General Staff Officer 1st Grade
2	2nd Grade
3	3rd Grade
GSP	Good Service Pension
GSR	Gun Sound Ranging
GSRS	General Support Rocket System
GSVAD	General Service Volunteer Aid Detachment
GSW	General Service Wagon
	Gunshot Wound
GTR	Gurkha Transport Regiment
GTS	Glider Training School

	Gunnery Training School
GW	Guided Weapon
	Guided Wire
GWpSO	Group Weapons Staff Officer
GYC	Glasgow Yeomanry Cavalry
H	Height Taker
	Horse
	Hussars
HA	Heavy Artillery
	High Angle
	Horse Artillery
	Hostile Aeroplane
	Hydrophone Allowance
HAA	Heavy Anti-Aircraft
HAC	Honourable Artillery Company
HACS	High Angle Control System
HAFB	Heavy Assault Floating Bridge
HALA	High Angle/Low Angle
HALO	High Altitude Low Opening
HAP	Hampshire Aircraft Parks
HAS	Hardened Aircraft Shelter
HASC	Hyderabad Army Service Corps
HASE	Head Angulation Sighting Equipment
HAST	High Altitude Selection Test
HAT	Heavy Artillery Tractor
Hav	Havildar
Hav-Maj	Havildar-Major
HB	Heavy Bomber
	Hinged Block
	Household Battalion
HBLO	Home Base, Ledger Office
HBM	Her/His Britannic Majesty
HB(N)	Heavy Bomber (Night)
HC	High Capacity [Bomb]
	Highland Cyclists
	Cross of Honour
	Household Cavalry
	Hyderabad Contingent
HCA	Hyderabad Contingent Artillery
HCB	Highland Cyclist Battalion
HCC	Hospital Conveyance Corps
	Hyderabad Contingent Cavalry
HCL	Hyderabad Contingent Lancers
HCO	Helicopter Control Officer
HCR	Household Cavalry Regiment

HCRR	Home Counties Reserve Regiment
HCT	High Commission Territories Corps
HCU	Heavy Conversion Unit
HD	Highland Division
	Home Defence
HDML	Harbour Defence Motor Launch
Hdqrs	Headquarters
HDU	Home Defence Unit
HE	High Explosive
	Hydrophone Effect
HEAP	High Explosive Armour-Piercing
HEAT	High Explosive Anti-Tank
HEIC	Honourable East India Company
HEICN	Honourable East India Company Navy
HEICS	Honourable East India Company's Service
HESH	High Explosive Squash Head
HET	Higher Educational Test
HE/T	High Explosive/Tracer
HF	Home Fleet
HFC	Higher Fire Control
HFDF	High Frequency Direction Finding
HFF	Heavy Freight Flight
HG	Home Guard
	Horse Guards
	Hotchkiss Gunner
HGCU	Heavy Glider Conversion Unit
HGMU	Heavy Glider Maintenance Unit
HH	Hodgson's Horse
HHNC	His Highness the Nizam's Cavalry
HI	Health Inspector
HIST	Hyderabad Imperial Service Troops
HIY	Hampshire Imperial Yeomanry
	Hertfordshire Imperial Yeomanry
HKMSC	Hong Kong Military Service Corps
HKR	Hong Kong Regiment
HKSRA	Hong Kong and Singapore Royal Artillery
HKSRGA	Hong Kong & Singapore Royal Garrison Artillery
HKVC	Hong Kong Volunteer Corps
HL	Hariana Lancers
HLH	Hertfordshire Light Horse
HLI	Highland Light Infantry
HLM	Hampshire Local Militia
	Hard-Lying Money
HM	Huntingdon Militia
HMA	His Majesty's Airship
HMAC	Her/His Majesty's Aircraft Carrier

51

HMAS	Her/His Majesty's Australian Ship
HMAV	Her/His Majesty's Army Vessel
HMB	Hazara Mountain Battery
HMBDV	Her/His Majesty's Boom Defence Vessel
HMCS	Her/His Majesty's Canadian Ship
HMD	Her/His Majesty's Destroyer
HMF	Her/His Majesty's Forces
HMG	Heavy Machine Gun
HMHS	Her/His Majesty's Hospital Ship
HMIS	Her/His Majesty's Indian Ship
HMLC	High Mobility Load Carrier
HMML	Her/His Majesty's Motor Launch
HMMMS	Her/His Majesty's Motor Mine Sweeper
HMNZS	Her/His Majesty's New Zealand Ship
HMRR	Her Majesty's Reserve Regiment
HMS	Her/His Majesty's Service
	Her/His Majesty's Ship
	Her/His Majesty's Steamer
HMS/M	Her/His Majesty's Submarine
HMT	Her/His Majesty's Transport
	Her/His Majesty's Trawler
	Her/His Majesty's Tug
	Her/His Majesty's Troopship
HO	Home Only
	Hostilities Only
HOMP	Halifax Ocean Meeting Point
HOT	Haut Subsonique Optiquement Teleguide¡Tire d'un Tube
How	Howitzer
Howr	Howitzer
HP	Handley-Page
	Health Physicist
hp	half-pay
HPER	Hastings & Prince Edward Regiment
HQ	Headquarters
HQBA	Headquarters Base Area
HQS	Headquarters Staff
HR	Halton Rifles
	Highland Regiment
Hr	Hussar
HRE	Hydro Reconnaissance Experimental
HS	Hospital Surgeon
H/S	High Speed
HSD	Higher Anti-Submarine Detector
HSF	High Seas Fleet
	Hyderabad State Force
HSL	High Speed Launch

HSMGC	Heavy Section Machine Gun Corps
HT	Horse Transport
HTD	Higher Telegraphist Detector
HVR	Hyderabad Volunteer Rifles
HW	Heavy Weapons
HY	Hertfordshire Yeomanry
HYC	Hampshire Yeomanry Cavalry
	Hertfordshire Yeomanry Cavalry
Hydr	Hydrographer
I	Intelligence
	Interpreter
IA	Indian Army
	Indian Artillery
	Instructional Allowance
IAA	Indian Army Act
IAC	Indian Army Circular
IAF	Independent Air Force
	Indian Air Force
	Indian Army Form
	Indian Auxiliary Force
IAFVH	Indian Advanced Field Veterinary Hospital
IAM	Institute of Aviation Medicine
IAMC	Indian Army Medical Corps
IOA	Indian Army Order
IAOC	Indian Army Ordnance Corps
IARO	Indian Army Reserve of Officers
IAS	Indicated Air Speed
	Inspector of Army Schools
IASC	Indian Army Service Corps
IAVC	Indian Army Veterinary Corps
IB	Incendiary Bomb
	Infantry Brigade
IBC	Imperial Bushmen Contingent
IBDVS	Indian Base Depot Veterinary Stores
IC	Instructor in Cookery
	Intelligence Corps
	Internal Combustion
	Irregular Cavalry
i/c	in charge
ICBM	Inter-Continental Ballistic Missile
ICC	Imperial Camel Corps
IC & CY	Inns of Court & City Yeomanry
ICO	Indian Commissioned Officer
ICOMP	Iceland Ocean Meeting Point
ICV	Infantry Combat Vehicle

IDC	Imperial Defence College
IDG	Inniskilling Dragoon Guards
IDR	Industrial Damage Report
	Infantry Drill Regulations
IDSM	Indian Distinguished Service Medal
IE	Initial Establishment
IED	Improvised Explosive Device
IEF	Indian Expeditionary Force
IEME	Corps of Indian Electrical & Mechanical Engineers
IF	Independent Force
	Irish Fusiliers
IFCS	Improved Fire Control System
IFDVS	Indian Field Depot Veterinary Stores
IFF	Identification Friend or Foe
IFVH	Indian Field Veterinary Hospital
IG	Inspector-General
	Instructor of Gunnery
	Irish Guards
IGC	Inspector-General of Communications
IGF	Inspector-General of Fortifications
IGT	Inspector-General of Transportation
IH	Irish Horse
IHC	Indian Hospital Corps
ILH	Imperial Light Horse
ILL	Illustrator
IMA	Indian Military Academy
IMB	Independent Mortar Battery
	Indian Mountain Battery
IMD	Indian Medical Department
Impl	Imperial
Impt	Imprisonment
IMR	Imperial Military Railways
IMS	Indian Medical Service
	Inshore Minesweeper
	International Military Staff
IMVH	Indian Military Veterinary Hospital
IMVS	Indian Mobile Veterinary Stores
In	Instructor
INAS	Inertial Navigation & Attack System
Inf	Infantry
Infty	Infantry
Infy	Infantry
INM	Institute of Naval Medicine
Int	Intelligence
INTSUM	Intelligence Summary
IO	Indian Officer

	Infantry Officer
	Intelligence Officer
I of A	Instructor of Artillery
I of M	Instructor of Musketry
IOM	Indian Order of Merit
	Inspector of Ordnance Machinery
IOO	Inspecting Ordnance Officer
IOR	Indian Other Rank
IP	Indian Pattern
IPC	Intelligence Priorities Committee
IR	Immediate Reserve
	Initial Reserve
	Infra-Red
IRBM	Intermediate Range Ballistic Missile
IRTD	Infantry Reinforcement Training Depot
IRV	Inglewood [Forest] Rifle Volunteers
IRVC	Indian Remount & Veterinary Corps
IS	Internal Security
ISC	Indian Staff Corps
	Inter-Service Communication
ISD	Indian Stores Depot
ISF	Indian States Force
ISMD	Indian Subordinate Medical Department
ISRM	Inter-Services Radio Measurements
ISS	Imperial Service Sappers
ISSB	Inter-Services Security Board
ISSU	Inter-Services Signals Unit
ISTDL	Inter-Services Training & Development Centre
ITC	Infantry Training Centre
ITDU	Infantry Trials & Development Unit
ITF	Indian Territorial Force
ITFMC	Indian Territorial Force Medical Corps
ITS	Initial Training School
ITW	Initial Training Wing
IUL	Indian Unattached List
IV	Irish Volunteers
IVCD	Indian Veterinary Convalescent Depot
IVH	Indian Veterinary Hospital
IW	Individual Weapon
IWC	Imperial War Cabinet
IWGC	Imperial War Graves Commission
IWHSD	Irish War Hospital Supply Depot
IWM	Imperial War Museum
IWR	Isle of Wight Rifles
IWT	Inland Water Transport
IY	Imperial Yeomanry

IYB	Imperial Yeomanry Bearer Corps
IYH	Imperial Yeomanry Hospital
JAAOC	Joint Anti-Aircraft Operation Centre
JACK	Junior Assistant Cook
JAF	Judge Advocate of the Fleet
JAG	Judge Advocate-General
JAKFORCE	Jammu & Kashmir Force
JANAP	Joint Army-Navy-Air Procedure
JAPC	Joint Air-Photo Centre
JARIC	Joint Air Reconnaissance Intelligence Centre
JARC	Joint Air Reconnaissance Centre
JASA	Junior Assistant Stores Accountant
JASS	Joint Anti-Submarine School
JASTD	Junior Assistant Steward
JATE	Joint Air Transport Establishment
JATO	Jet Assisted Take-Off
JATP	Joint Air Training Plan
JAWTR	Junior Assistant Writer
JCA	Junior Catering Accountant
JCC	Joint Communications Centre
	Junior Command Course
JCD	John Chard Decoration
JCE	Joint Cadet Executive
JCEM	Junior Control Electrical Mechanic
JCOC	Joint Command Operations Centre
J/CSM	Junior Company Sergeant-Major
JD	Junior Division
JDS	Joint Defence Staff
JEHU	Joint Experimental Helicopter Unit
JEM(A)1	Junior Electrical Mechanic (Air) 1st class
2	2nd class
JEM(AW)1	Junior Electrical Mechanic (Air Weapon) 1st class
2	2nd class
Jem	Jemadar
JEWT	Jungle Exercise Without Trees
JFS	Jane's Fighting Ships
J/Gdsmn	Junior Guardsman
JH	Jacob's Horse
JHQ	Joint Headquarters
JIC	Joint Intelligence Committee
JIS	Joint Intelligence Staff
JL	Junior Leaders Regiment
J/L/Cpl	Junior Lance-Corporal
J/Ldr	Junior Leader
J/L/Sgt	Junior Lance-Sergeant

JLR	Junior Leaders Regiment
JMA	Junior Medical Assistant
JMEM	Junior Marine Engineering Mechanic
J/Mne	Junior Marine
JMR	Johannesburg Mounted Rifles
J/Musn	Junior Musician
JNA(1)	Junior Naval Airman 1st class
(2)	2nd class
JNAM	Junior Naval Air Mechanic
JNCO	Junior Non-Commissioned Officer
JOC	Joint Operations Centre
JOEM	Junior Ordnance Electrical Mechanic
JPC	Joint Planning Committee
JPRO	Joint Photographic Reconnaissance Organisation
JPS	Joint Planning Staff
JREM	Junior Radio Electrical Mechanic
JRO	Junior Radio Operator
J/RSM	Junior Regimental Sergeant-Major
JS	Joint Services
	Junior Seaman
JSC	Joint Chiefs of Staff
JSLS	Joint Services Liaison Staff
JSSC	Joint Services Staff College
JTC	Junior Training Corps
JUO	Junior Under-Officer
JWE	Joint Warfare Establishment
JWS	Joint Warfare Staff
KA	HMS King Alfred
KAPE	Keeping the Army in the Public Eye
KAR	King's African Rifles
KC	King's Colonials
KCIO	King's Commissioned Indian Officer
KCLY	Kent & County of London Yeomanry
KCYC	King's Cheshire Yeomanry Cavalry
KD	Khaki Drill
KDG	King's Dragoon Guards
KEH	King Edward's Horse
KEO	King Edward's Own
KEOC	King Edward's Own Cavalry
KEOL	King Edward's Own Lancers
KEV	King's Empire Veterans
KG5	HMS King George V
KGA	King's German Artillery
KGL	King's German Legion
KGO	King's Gurkha Officer

KGVO	King George the Fifth's Own
KH	King's Hussars
	Kneller Hall
KHM	King's Harbour Master
KIA	Killed in Action
KIS	Kenya Independent Squadron
KLD	King's Light Dragoons
KLI	King's Light Infantry (Shropshire)
KM	King's Medal
	Kurram Militia
KMR	Kafrarian Mounted Rifles
KN	Kenya Navy
KOB	King's Own Borderers
KODR	King's Overseas Dominions Regiment
KOH	King's Own Hussars
KOLI	King's Own Light Infantry
KORR	King's Own Royal Regiment
KOSB	King's Own Scottish Borderers
KOYLI	King's Own Yorkshire Light Infantry
KR	King's Regiment
KR & ACI	King's Regulations and Air Council Instructions
KR & AI	King's Regulations and Admiralty Instructions
KRIH	King's Royal Irish Hussars
KRRC	King's Royal Rifle Corps
KSLI	King's Shropshire Light Infantry
KUA	Kit Upkeep Allowance
KVF	Kent Volunteer Fencibles
KY	Kent Yeomanry
L	Electrical
	Lancers
	Layer
	Lieutenant
LA	Leading Airman
	Lodging Allowance
LAA	Lieutenant-at-Arms
	Light Anti-Aircraft
LAB	Low Altitude Bombing
LAC	Leading Aircraftman
LACMN	Leading Aircrewman
LACW	Leading Aircraftwoman
LAD	Light Aid Detachment
LADA	London Air Defence Area
LAFB	Light Assault Floating Bridge
LAFV	Light Armoured Fighting Vehicle
LAM	Leading Air Mechanic

LAMB	Light Armoured Motor Brigade
LAPADS	Lightweight Acoustic Processing and Display System
LASU	Local Air Supply Unit
LAT	Light Artillery Tractor
LAW	Light Anti-tank Weapon
	Light Assault Weapon
LB	Light Battalion
	Light Bomber
LBC	Lothian & Berwick Cavalry
L/Bdr	Lance-Bombardier
LBE	Landing Barge Emergency Repair
LBF	Landing Barge Flak
L & B Horse	Lothians & Border Horse
LBK	Landing Barge Kitchen
LBO	Landing Barge Oiler
LBTI	Long-Burning Target Indicator
LBV	Landing Barge Vehicle
LBW	Landing Barge Water
LC	Labour Corps
	Landing Craft
	Light Company
L/C	Lance-Corporal
LCA	Landing Craft Assault
	Leading Catering Accountant
LCA(FT)	Landing Craft Assault (Flamethrower)
LCA(HR)	Landing Craft Assault (Hedgerow)
LCA(OC)	Landing Craft Assault (Obstacle Clearance)
LCC	Landing Craft Control
LCE	Landing Craft Emergency Repairs
LCEM	Leading Control Electrical Mechanic
LCF	Landing Craft Flak
LC(FF)	Landing Craft (Flotilla Flagship).
LCG(L)	Landing Craft Gun (Large)
LCG(M)	Landing Craft Gun (Medium)
LCG(S)	Landing Craft Gun (Small)
LCH	Landing Craft Headquarters
	Landing Craft Hospital
Lchr	Launcher
LCI	Landing Craft Infantry
LCI(D)	Landing Craft Infantry (Demolition)
LCI(G)	Landing Craft Infantry (Gun)
LCI(L)	Landing Craft Infantry (Large)
LCI(M)	Landing Craft Infantry (Medium)
	Landing Craft Infantry (Mortar)
LCI(R)	Landing Craft Infantry (Rocket)
LCI(S)	Landing Craft Infantry (Small)

LCK	Landing Craft Kitchen
L Ck	Leading Cook
LCL	Landing Craft Logistic
LCM	Landing Craft Mechanised
LCM(G)	Landing Craft Mechanised (Gun)
LCMP	Local Commandant Military Police
LCM(R)	Landing Craft Mechanised (Rocket)
LCN	Landing Craft Navigation
LCO	Landing Craft Officer
LCOCU	Landing Craft Obstacle Clearance Unit
L/COH	Lance-Corporal of Horse
L Col	Lieutenant Colonel
L/Corp	Lance-Corporal
L/Cpl	Lance-Corporal
LCP	Landing Craft Personnel
LCP(L)	Landing Craft Personnel (Large)
LCP(M)	Landing Craft Personnel (Medium)
LCP(N)	Landing Craft Personnel (Nested)
LCP(R)	Landing Craft Personnel (Ramped)
LCP(S)	Landing Craft Personnel (Small)
LCP(Sy)	Landing Craft Personnel (Survey)
LCP(U)	Landing Craft Personnel (Utility)
LCR	Landing Craft Raiding
	Landing Craft Rocket
L Cr	Lieutenant-Commander
LCR(L)	Landing Craft Rubber (Large)
LCR(S)	Landing Craft Rubber (Small)
LCS	Landing Craft Support
	Light Cruiser Squadron
	London Controlling Section
LCS(L)	Landing Craft Support (Large)
LCS(M)	Landing Craft Support (Medium)
LCS(R)	Landing Craft Support (Rocket)
LCS(S)	Landing Craft Support (Small)
LCT	Landing Craft Tank
LCT(A)	Landing Craft Tank (Armoured)
LCT(H)	Landing Craft Tank (Hospital)
LCT(R)	Landing Craft Tank (Rocket)
LCU	Landing Craft Utility
LCV	Landing Craft Vehicles
	Lorry Command Vehicle
LCVP	Landing Craft Vehicles & Personnel
LD	Light Dragoons
LDA	Lower-Deck Attitude
LDV	Local Defence Volunteers
LDY	Leicestershire & Derbyshire Yeomanry (Prince Albert's Own)

LE	Lee-Enfield
LEM(A)	Leading Electrical Mechanic (Air)
LEM(AW)	Leading Electrical Mechanic (Air Weapon)
LEP	Locally Enlisted Personnel
LEV	Loyal Edinburgh Volunteers
LF	Lancashire Fusiliers
	Legion of Frontiersmen
LFB	Light Field Battery
LFS	Lancaster Finishing School
LFSS	Landing Force Support Ship
LG	Landing Ground
	Large Grain
	Lewis Gun(ner)
	Life Guards
LgA	Lodging Allowance
LGE	Landing Ground, Emergency
L Gen	Lieutenant-General
LH	Light Horse
	Loch's Horse
LHA	Lord High Admiral
LHV	Light Horse Volunteers
LHY	Lancashire Hussars Yeomanry
LI	Light Infantry
LIAP	Leave in Addition to Python
Lieut	Lieutenant
Lieut-Col	Lieutenant-Colonel
Lieut-Gen	Lieutenant-General
LILOP	Leave in Lieu of Python
LISV	Loyal Independent Sheffield Volunteers
LIV	Light Infantry Volunteers
LIVEX	Live Exercise
LIY	Leicestershire Imperial Yeomanry
L/L	Leigh Light
LLH	Lahore Light Horse
LLL	Loyal Lusitanian League
LLV	Loyal London Volunteers
LM	Lee-Metford
	Local Militia
LMA	Leading Medical Assistant
LMF	Lack of Moral Fibre
LMG	Light Machine Gun
LMLE	Long Magazine Lee-Enfield
LMR	Longmoor Military Railway
LnA	London Allowance
L/Nk	Lance-Naik
LNSF	Light Night Striking Force

LO	Liaison Officer
LOA	Local Overseas Allowance
LOB	Left Out of Battle
LOEM(A)	Leading Ordnance Electrical Mechanic (Air)
L of C	Line(s) of Communication
LOGEX	Logistics Exercise
LOH	Oxfordshire Light Horse
LORAN	Long Range Air Navigation System
	Long Range Navigation System
LOSAM	Low Altitude Surface-to-Air Missile
LP	Landing Point
L & PA	Lodging & Pay Allowance
LPD	Landing Platform Dock
LPH	Landing Platform Helicopter
LPT	Leading Physical Trainer
LR	Layer Rating
	Loyal Regiment
Lr	Lancer
L/R	Long Range
LRATGW	Long Range Anti-Tank Guided Weapon
LRB	London Rifle Brigade
LRDG	Long Range Desert Group
LREG	Leading Regulator
LREM(A)	Leading Radio Electrical Mechanic (Air)
LRO	Leading Radio Operator
LRF	Laser Rangefinder
LRMP	Long Range Maritime Patrol
LRMTS	Laser Ranger & Marked Target Selector
L/RO	Leading Radio Operator
LRO(G)	Leading Radio Operator (General)
(W)	(Warfare)
LRP	Long Range Patrol
	Long Range Penetration
LRR	Long Range Rocket
LRS	Light Repair Section
LRV	Lanarkshire Rifle Volunteers
	Lancashire Rifle Volunteers
LS	Land Service
	Leading Seaman
	Le Gros Scouts
	Long Service
	Lovat Scouts
LSA	Leading Stores Accountant
LSB	Landing Ship Bombardment
LSC	Landing Ship Carrier
LSCC	London Scottish Cadet Corps

LSD	Landing Ship Dock
LSE	Landing Ship Emergency Repair
LSF	Landing Ship Fighter Direction
LSG	Landing Ship Gantry
	Landing Ship Gun
LS & GC	Long Service & Good Conduct
L/Sgt	Lance Sergeant
LSH	Landing Ship Headquarters
	Loyal Suffolk Hussars
LSHQ	Landing Ship Headquarters
LSI(H)	Landing Ship Infantry (Hand-hoisting)
LSI(L)	Landing Ship Infantry (Large)
LSI(M)	Landing Ship Infantry (Medium)
LSI(S)	Landing Ship Infantry (Small)
LSL	Landing Ship Logistic
LSM	Landing Ship Medium
L/Smn	Leading Seaman
LSM(R)	Landing Ship Medium (Rocket)
LSP	Landing Ship Personnel
LSR	Landing Ship Rocket
LSRV	London Scottish Rifle Volunteers
LSS	Landing Ship Sternchute
	Landing Ship Support
LST	Landing Ship Tank
LST(H)	Landing Ship Tank (Hospital)
LSTD	Leading Steward
LSV	Landing Ship Vehicle
LSW	Light Support Weapon
LT	Loader-Transporter
	Leading Telegraphist
Lt	Lieutenant
L/T	Line Telegraphy
LTC	Land Transport Corps
Lt-Cdr	Lieutenant-Commander
Lt-Col	Lieutenant-Colonel
Lt-Comm	Lieutenant-Commander
LTF	Lightning Training Flight
Lt-Gen	Lieutenant-General
Lt Inf	Light Infantry
LTO	Leading Torpedoman
LTR	Long Term Reserve
LUC	Living Under Canvas
LUOTC	London University Officers Training Corps
LUP	Laying-Up Position
LUSCC	Latymer Upper School Cadet Corps
LV	Lancastrian Volunteers

	Leeds Volunteers
	Light Vehicle
	Low Velocity
LVA	Lancashire Volunteer Artillery
LVR	London Volunteer Regiment
LVT	Landing Vehicle, Tracked
LVT(A)	Landing Vehicle, Tracked (Armoured)
LVTP	Landing Vehicle, Tracked, Personnel
LVT(R)	Landing Vehicle, Tracked (Rocket)
LVW	Landing Vehicle, Wheeled
LWRENAM	Leading Wren Air Mechanic
LWRENCINE	Leading Wren Cinema Operator
LWRENDSA	Leading Wren Dental Surgery Assistant
LWRENDHYG	Leading Wren Dental Hygienist
LWRENEDUC	Leading Wren Education Assistant
LWRENHAIR	Leading Wren Hairdresser
LWRENMET	Leading Wren Mereorologist
LWRENMT	Leading Wren Motor Transport Driver
LWRENPHOT	Leading Wren Photographer
LWRENQA	Leading Wren Quarters Assistant
LWRENREM	Leading Wren Radio Electrical Mechanic
LWRENRO(M)	Leading Wren Radio Operator (Morse)
LWRENS(C)	Leading Wren Stores Assistant (Clothes)
LWRENS(S)	Leading Wren Stores Assistant (Stores)
LWRENS(V)	Leading Wren Stores Assistant (Victualling)
LWRENSTD	Leading Wren Steward
LWRENTEL	Leading Wren Telephonist
LWRENTSA	Leading Wren Training Support Assistant
LWRENWA	Leading Wren Weapon Analyst
LWRENWTR(G)	Leading Wren Writer (General)
LWRENWTR(P)	Leading Wren Writer (Pay)
LWRENWTR(S)	Leading Wren Writer (Shorthand)
LWTR	Leading Writer
LY	Leicestershire Yeomanry (Prince Albert's Own)
	Queen's Own Lowland Yeomanry
LYC	Leicestershire Yeomanry Cavalry (Prince Albert's Own)
LZ	Landing Zone
LZL	Launcher, Zero Length
M	Matron
	Marksman
	Mechanician
	Militia
	Moulder
MA	Madras Artillery
	Master Assistant

	Mechanician Apprentice
	Medical Assistant
	Messing Allowance
	Military Accountant
	Military Administration
	Military Attache
	Mountain Artillery
	Munitions Australia
MAA	Master-at-Arms
MAAF	Mediterranean Allied Air Forces
MAC	Mediterranean Air Command
	Merchant Aircraft Carrier
	Military Aid to the Community
	Motor Ambulance Convoy
MACAF	Mediterranean Allied Coastal Air Force
MACC	Military Aid to the Civil Community
MACM	Military Aid to Civil Ministries
MACP	Military Aid to the Civil Power
MAD	Magnetic Anomaly Detector
MAFP	Military & Air Force Police
Maj	Major
Maj-Gen	Major-General
MANHC	Madras Army Native Hospital Corps
MAP	Ministry of Aircraft Production
MAPRC	Mediterranean Airforces Photographic Reconnaissance Centre
MARAIRMED	Maritime Air Forces, Mediterranean
MARCONFOR	Maritime Contingency Force
MARCONFOR-LANT	Maritime Contingency Force, Atlantic
MARITA	Maritime Airfield
MAS	Military Agency for Standardisation
MASAF	Mediterranean Allied Strategic Air Force
MASB	Motor Anti-Submarine Boat
MASTU	Mobile Anti-Submarine Training Unit
MAT	Medium Artillery Tractor
MATAF	Mediterranean Allied Tactical Air Force
MATC	Mountain Artillery Training Centre
MATCH	Medium-range Anti-submarine Torpedo-Carrying Helicopter
MATO	Military Air Traffic Operations
MATS	Model Aircraft Target System
M & AW	Mountain & Arctic Warfare
MB	Medium Bomber
	Motor Boatman
	Mountain Battery

MBC	Malwa Bhil Corps
	Mewar Bhil Corps
	Motorboat Crew
MBFR	Mutual & Balanced Force Reductions
MBK	Missing Believed Killed
MBS	Muzzle Bore Sight
MBT	Main Battle Tank
MC	Marine Craft
	Medium Capacity [Bomb]
	Medium Charge
	Military Cross
	Mine Clearance
	Mortar Carrier
	Motorcycle Driver
	Movement Control
MCD	Mine Warfare & Clearance Diving
MCM	Mine Counter-Measures
MCMV	Mine-Counter-Measures Vessel
MCO	Movement Control Officer
MCoS	Military College of Science
MCRI	Marine Craft Radio Installation
MCS	Metropolitan Communications Squadron
	Mine Counter-measures Ship
	Movements Control Section
MCSC	Magdalen College School Cadets
MCTD	Medium Capacity Bomb with Temporary Delay Fuse
MCU	Mosquito Conversion Unit
MCV	Mechanized Combat Vehicle
MD	Medical Department
	Mess Deck
	Military District
	Modified Design [Cordite]
M & D	Medicine & Duty
MDC	Mobile Defence Corps
MDCH	Duke of Cambridge's Middlesex Yeomanry Hussars
MDG	Medical Director-General
MDS	Magnetic Detection of Submarines
	Main Dressing Station
MDW	Mine Disposal Weapon
ME	Marine Engineer
	Martini Enfield
	Metalsmith
MEA	Marine Engineering Artificer
MEAF	Middle East Air Force
MEC	Medical Examination Centre
MECH	Mechanician

MEF	Mediterranean Expeditionary Force
	Middle East Force
MEIC	Middle East Intelligence Centre
MELF	Middle East Land Forces
MEM	Marine Engineering Mechanic
MEO	Marine Engineer Officer
	Mining Engineering Officer
MEOOW	Marine Engineer Officer of the Watch
MEOW	Marine Engineer Officer's Writer
MER	Madras European Regiment
MESA	Mobile Entertainments Southern Area
Met	Meteorological
METCAL	Meteorological Calibration
Meth Ch	Methodist Chaplain
MEW	Ministry of Economic Warfare
	Mobile Early Warning
MEWC	Middle East War Council
MExB	Motor Explosive Boat
MEXE	Military Engineering Experimental Establishment
MF	Maurice-Farman
	Royal Munster Fusiliers
MFD	Military Forwarding Depot
MFE	Manual of Field Engineering
MFH	Mobile Field Hospital
MFO	Military Forwarding Officer
MFB	Military Foot Police
MFV	Motor Fishing Vessel
MG	Machine Gun
	Machine Gunner
MGB	Medium Girder Bridge
	Motor Gunboat
MGC	Machine Gun Corps
MGG	Machine Gun Guards
MGO	Machine Gun Officer
	Master-General of Ordnance
MGR	Machine Gun Regiment
MGRI	Mobile Ground Radio Installation
MGRM	Major-General Royal Marines
MGS	Machine Gun School
MH	Martini Henry
	Middlesex Hussars (Duke of Cambridge's)
	Military Hospital
MHQ	Maritime Headquarters
MHS	Military Historical Society
MI	Medical Inspection
	Military Intelligence

	Mounted Infantry
	Movement Instruction
MIA	Missing in Action
MICV	Mechanised Infantry Combat Vehicle
MID	Mentioned in Dispatches
	Munitions Inventions Department
Mid	Midshipman
Mil	Military
	Militia
Mila	Militia
MILAN	Missile d'Infanterie Leger Antichar
M-in-C	Matron-in-Chief
MIO	Military Intelligence Officer
MIRV	Multi-Independently Targeted Re-entry Vehicle
MIY	Montgomeryshire Imperial Yeomanry
MJL	Murray's Jat Lancers
Mk	Mark
ML	Madras Lancers
	Motor Launch
	Mountain Leader
	Muzzle Loader
M/L	Minelayer
MLA	Motor Launch, Auxiliary
MLC	Madras Light Cavalry
MLE	Magazine Lee-Enfield
MLF	Multilateral Force
MLI	Maltese Light Infantry
MLM	Magazine Lee-Metford
MLNS	Ministry of Labour & National Service
MLO	Military Landing Officer
MLR	Muzzle-Loading Rifle
MLRG	Muzzle-Loading Rifled Gun
MLRS	Multiple Launch Rocket System
MLS	Minimum Launch Speed
MLT	Medium Level Tripod
MM	Military Medal
	Ministry of Munitions
	Motor Mechanic
MMG	Medium Machine Gun
	Motor Machine Gun Corps
MMGB	Motor Machine Gun Battalion
MMGS	Motor Machine Gun Service
MMIA	Military Mission to the Italian Army
MML	Manual of Military Law
MMP	Mashonaland Mounted Police
	Matabeleland Mounted Police

	Military Mounted Police
MMS	Military Message Service
	Motor Minesweeper
MNB	Mobile Naval Base
MNBDO	Mobile Naval Base Defence Organization
Mne	Marine
MNI	Madras Native Infantry
MO	Medical Officer
	Military Operations
MOA	Marine Officer's Attendant
MOBAT	Mobile Battalion Anti-Tank Gun
MOD	Ministry of Defence
MOIC	Medical Officer in Charge
MOLCAB	Mobile Landing Craft Advanced Base
MOMP	Mid-Ocean Meeting Point
MONAB	Mobile Naval Advanced Base
Mor	Mortar
MOVCO	Movement Control Organization
MOVREP	Movement Report
MOWT	Ministry of War Transport
MP	Marine Provost
	Military Police
MPD	Military Prisons Department
MPFC	Mobile Petrol Filling Centre
MPI	Mean Point of Impact
MPSC	Military Provost Staff Corps
MR	Map Reference
	Maritime Reconnaissance
	Master
	Middlesex Regiment
	Militia Reserve
M/R	Medium Range
MRA	Maritime Royal Artillery
MRAF	Marshal of the Royal Air Force
MRBM	Medium-Range Ballistic Missile
MRCA	Multi-Role Combat Aircraft
MRCP	Mobile Radar Control Post
MRE	Militia Royal Engineers
MRF	Military Reconnaissance Force
MRG	Main Repair Group
MRS	Military Railway Services
	Muzzle Reference System
MRU	Maritime Reconnaissance Unit
	Mobile Radio Unit
MS	Medical Services
	Medical Staff

	Military Secretary
	Military Staff
M/S	Minesweeper
MSA	Military Service Act
MSC	Madras Staff Corps
	Medical Staff Corps
	Minesweeper, Coastal
MSD	Military Store Department
MSF	Minesweeper, Fleet
MSFU	Merchant Service Fighter Unit
MSI	Minesweeper, Inshore
MSL	Minesweeping Launch
	Missile
MSM	Meritorious Service Medal
	Minesweeper, Medium
MSMD	Madras Subordinate Medical Department
MSO	Minesweeper, Ocean
	Mixed Services Organization
MSR	Maintenance Supply Route
MSRD	Mobile Servicing Repair Detachment
MSSC	Military Store Staff Corps
MSU	Mobile Signals Unit
MT	Mechanical Traction
	Mechanical Transport
	Medical Technician
	Military Train
	Motor Driver
	Motor Transport
MTA 4	Medical Technician, Acting, 4th class
MTB	Motor Torpedo Boat
MTC	Mechanical Transport Corps
MTD	Mechanical Road Transport Driver
Mtd	Mounted
MTI	Military Training Instructor
	Moving Target Indicator
MTM	Mechanical Road Transport Mechanic
MTO	Motor Transport Officer
MTTC	Mechanised Transport Training Corps
MTU	Mosquito Training Unit
MTV	Motor Transport Volunteers
MU	Maintenance Unit
MU/AG	Mid-Upper [Turret] Air Gunner
Musn	Musician
MV	Motor Vessel
	Motor Volunteers
	Muzzle Velocity

M & V	Meat & Vegetables [Tinned]
MVC	Motor Volunteer Corps
MVEE	Military Vehicles Engineering Establishment
MW	Metalworker
MWEE	Mechanised Warfare Experimental Establishment
MVR	Malabar Volunteer Rifles
	Mussoorie Volunteer Rifles
MW	Mine Warfare
MWA	Munitions of War Act
MWT	Ministry of War Transport
MXRV	Middlesex Rifle Volunteers
MXVRC	Middlesex Volunteer Rifle Corps
MY	Montgomeryshire Yeomanry
MYC	Middlesex Yeomanry Cavalry
	Montgomeryshire Yeomanry Cavalry
N	Naval
NA	Naval Attache
N/A	No Action
	Not Available
NA 1	Naval Airman 1st class
2	2nd class
NA 1SL	Naval Assistant to the First Sea Lord
NAA	National Artillery Association
NAAF	North-west African Air Forces
NAAFI	Navy, Army & Air Force Institutes
NAASC	North-west African Air Service Command
NAC	Naval Air Command
NACAF	North-west African Coastal Air Force
NACB	Navy & Army Canteen Board
NAD	Naval Air Division
	No Appreciable Disease
NADC	Naval Aide-de-camp
NADEFCOL	NATO Defence College
NADGE	NATO Air Defence Ground Environment
NAM	National Army Museum
	Naval Air Mechanic
NAMET	Naval Mathematics & English Test
NAMFI	NATO Missile Firing Installation
NAP	Naval Auxiliary Patrol
NAPRW	North-west African Photographic Reconnaissance Wing
NAS	Naval Air Station
NASAF	North-west African Strategic Air Force
NATAF	North-west African Tactical Air Force
NATBF	North-west African Tactical Bomber Force
NATC	North-west African Training Command

NATCC	North-west African Troop Carrier Command
NATO	North Atlantic Treaty Organization
Nav	Navigator
NAVYEO	Navigator's Yeoman
NBC	Nuclear, Biological, Chemical Warfare
NBMR	Northern Bengal Mounted Rifles
NBS	Navigational Bombing System
NC	Natal Carabiniers
	Native Cavalry
NCAC	Northern Combat Area Command
NCC	Non-Combatant Corps
NCLC	Non-Combatant Labour Corps
NCMR	North Canterbury Mounted Rifles
NCO	Non-Commissioned Officer
NCPT	Navy Central Planning Team
NCS	Naval Canteen Service
	Naval Controller of Shipping
N CYC BN	Northern Cyclist Battalion
NDA	Naval Discipline Act
NDC	National Defence College
	National Defence Company
NDD	Navigation & Direction Division
NDF	Naval Defence Force
NDH	Royal North Devonshire Yeomanry Hussars
NDIY	North Devon Imperial Yeomanry
NDM	North Durham Militia
NE	Night Experimental
	Not Entitled
NEAF	Near East Air Force
NEARELF	Near East Land Forces
NEC	Northern European Command
NED	Naval Equipment Department
NES	Naval Examination Service
NF	Northumberland Fusiliers
N/F	Night Fighter
NFA	Natal Field Artillery
NFF	Natal Field Force
NFH	Native Field Hospital
NFOO	Naval Forward Observing Officer
NFPS	Naval Future Policy Staff
NG	Royal North Gloucestershire Militia
NGVC	National Guard Volunteer Corps
NGVR	New Guinea Volunteer Rifles
NH	Naval Hospital
	Northumberland Hussars
NHIY	Northumberland Hussars Imperial Yeomanry

NHY	Northumberland Hussars Yeomanry
NI	Native Infantry
	Naval Instructor
NID	Naval Intelligence Department
NIH	North Irish Horse
NILE	Naval Inflatable Life-saving Equipment
NIY	Northamptonshire Imperial Yeomanry
	Northumberland Imperial Yeomanry
Nk	Naik
NL	Navy League
	Navy List
NLD	Naval Electrical Department
NMB	Naval Meteorological Branch
NMC	Natal Medical Corps
NMM	National Maritime Museum
NMR	Natal Mounted Rifles
	National Military Representative
NM Volunteers	National Motor Volunteers
NMWC	Nelson, Marlborough & West Coast Regiment
NNC	Natal Native Contingent
NNH	Natal Native Horse
NO	Native Officer
	Naval Officer
NOD	Naval Ordnance Department
	Night Observation Device
NOGL	Nizam's Own Golgonda Lancers
NOIC	Naval Officer In Charge
NOK	Next of Kin
NORTHAG	Northern Army Group
NP	Naval Party
	Naval Patrol
	Naval Pattern
	Naval Pension
	New Pattern
NPAM	Non-Permanent Active Militia
NPC	Naval Personnel Committee
NR	National Reserve
	Nigeria Regiment
	Norfolk Rangers
NRA	National Rifle Association
NRD	Naval Recruiting Department
NRR	Northern Rhodesia Regiment
NRS	Naval Recruiting Service
NRV	Northamptonshire Rifle Volunteer Corps
NS	National Service
	Naval Stores

	North Somerset [Imperial Yeomanry]
	Nursing Sister
NSD	Naval Stores Department
NSE	National Support Elements
NSHQ	Naval Staff Headquarters
NSIY	North Somerset Imperial Yeomanry
NSL	National Service League
NSM	National Serviceman
NSO	National Service Officer
	Naval Staff Officer
NSR	Nova Scotia Regiment
NSWB	New South Wales Bushmen
NSY	North Salopian Yeomanry
	North Somerset Yeomanry
NTC	Nautical Training Corps
NTD	Naval Training Department
NTO	Naval Transport Officer
NVAC	Natal Voluntary Ambulance Corps
NVR	Norfolk Volunteer Regiment
NW	Nuclear Weapon
NWFP	North West Frontier Province
NY	Northamptonshire Yeomanry
	Northumberland Yeomanry
NYD	Not Yet Diagnosed
NZA	New Zealand Artillery
NZAAC	New Zealand Army Air Corps
NZAEC	New Zealand Army Educational Corps
NZAMC	New Zealand Army Medical Corps
NZANS	New Zealand Army Nursing Service
NZAOC	New Zealand Army Ordnance Corps
NZAPC	New Zealand Army Pay Corps
NZASC	New Zealand Army Service Corps
NZCC	New Zealand Cyclist Corps
NZCS	New Zealand Corps of Signals
NZDC	New Zealand Dental Corps
NZE	Corps of New Zealand Engineers
NZEF	New Zealand Expeditionary Force
NZEVA	New Zealand Empire Veterans Association
NZFA	New Zealand Field Artillery
NZGA	New Zealand Garrison Artillery
NZMC	New Zealand Medical Corps
NZMGC	New Zealand Machine Gun Corps
NZMGS	New Zealand Machine Gun Section
NZMP	New Zealand Military Police
NZMR	New Zealand Mounted Rifles
NZNC	New Zealand Native Contingent

NZOC	New Zealand Ordnance Corps
NZPS	New Zealand Permanent Staff
NZP & TC	New Zealand Post & Telegraph Corps
NZR	New Zealand Rifles
NZRB	New Zealand Rifle Brigade
NZRR	New Zealand Rough Riders
NZSAS	New Zealand Special Air Service
NZSC	New Zealand Staff Corps
NZSM	New Zealand Submarine Mining [Volunteers]
NZTS	New Zealand Temporary Staff
NZVC	New Zealand Veterinary Corps
	New Zealand Volunteer Corps
NZWRAC	New Zealand Women's Royal Army Corps
O	Observer
	Ordnance
OA	Officers Association
	Ordnance Artificer
OAPU	Overseas Air Preparation Unit
OARS	Ocean Area Reconnaissance Submarine
OAS	On Active Service
OB	Order of Burma
	Ordnance Board
OBC	Old Boys Corps
OBI	Order of British India
OBLI	Oxfordshire & Buckinghamshire Light Infantry
Obs Lt	Observer Lieutenant
OBU	Operational Base Unit
OC	Officer Commanding
	Officers Cook
O/C	Officer Cadet
OCA	Old Comrades Association
OCAC	Officer Commanding Administrative Centre
OCB	Officer Cadet Battalion
OCP	Officer Candidate Programme
OCRM	Officer Commanding Royal Marines
OCS	Officer Candidate School
OCTU	Officer Cadet Training Unit
OCU	Operational Conversion Unit
OD	Operations Division
	Ordinary Seaman
	Other Denomination
OE	Ordnance Electrician
	Ordnance Engineer
OEA	Ordnance Electrical Artificer
OELMN(A)	Ordnance Electrical Mechanician (Air)

OEM 1	Ordnance Electrical Mechanic 1st class
2	2nd class
OEMN 1	Ordnance Electrical Mechanician 1st class
2	2nd class
3	3rd class
OETA	Occupied Enemy Territories Administration
OF	Oil Fuel
OFA	Overseas Family Allowance
Offr	Officer
OFP	Ordnance Field Park
O Group	Orders Group
OH	Otago Hussars
OHBMS	On Her/His Britannic Majesty's Service
OHMS	On Her/His Majesty's Service
OHQ	Overseas Headquarters
OIC	Operational Intelligence Centre
O i/c	Officer in charge
OL	Ordnance Lieutenant
OL Cr	Ordnance Lieutenant-Commander
OLH	Orpen's Light Horse
	Oxfordshire Light Horse
OLQ	Officer-Like Qualities
OM	Observer's Mate
OMD	Ordnance Medical Department
OME	Ordnance Mechanical Engineer
OML	Ordnance Muzzle Loading
ONC	Optimists National Corps
Ont Rgt	Ontario Regiment
OO	Orderly Officer
	Ordnance Officer
OOB	Order of Battle
OOG	Officer of the Guard
OOW	Officer of the Watch
OOD	Officer of the Day
OP	Observation Post
	Old Pattern
Opl	Operational
OPRA	Observation Post Royal Artillery
OPMACC	Operation Military Aid to the Civil Community
Ops	Operations
OPSUM	Operational Summary
OR	Operational Requirements
	Operational Research
	Orderly Room
	Oswestry Rangers
	Other Rank

ORA	Operating Room Attendant
ORB	Operations Record Book
Ord	Ordnance
Ord Sgt	Ordnance Sergeant
ORQMC	Orderly Room Quartermaster-Corporal
ORQMS	Orderly Room Quartermaster-Sergeant
ORR Rifles	Oudh & Rohilkand Railway Rifles
ORS	Operational Research Section
	Orderly Room Sergeant
OS	Officers Steward
	Ordinary Seaman
OSA	Official Secrets Act
OSC	Ordnance Store Corps
OSD	Officers Service Dress
OSL	Ordnance Sub-Lieutenant
OTC	Officer in Tactical Command
	Officers Training Corps
	Officers Transit Camp
OTP	Oscillation Test Point
OTU	Operational Training Unit
OUMC	Otago University Medical Corps
OUVB	Oxford University Volunteer Battalion
OVR	Oudtshoorn Volunteer Rifles
OW	Officer's Writer
P	Paymaster
	Pebble
	Pilot
	Plotter
	Predictor
PA	Pakistan Army
	Prince Albert's
	Provision Allowance
Pa	Parachutist
P/AA 3	Probationary Aircraft Artificer 3rd class
P/AAA 2	Probationary Aircraft Artificer Acting 2nd class
PACD	Parachute and Cable Defence
P/ACEA 2	Probationary Control Electrical Artificer Acting 2nd class
PAD	Passive Air Defence
PADS	Position & Azimuth Determining System
PAEC	Pakistan Army Education Corps
PAG	Prince Albert's Guard
PAIC	Persia and Iraq Command
PAIFORCE	Persia and Iraq Force
PAMC	Pakistan Army Medical Corps
P/AMEA 2	Probationary Marine Engineering Artificer Acting 2nd class

77

PAO	Prince Albert's Own
PAOC	Pakistan Army Ordnance Corps
P/AOEA 2	Probationary Ordnance Electrical Artificer Acting 2nd class
PAPTC	Pakistan Army Physical Training Corps
P/AREA	Probationary Acting Radio Electrical Artificer
PASO	Principal Armament Supply Officer
PASWEPS	Passive Anti-Submarine Warfare Environmental Protection Scheme
PATO	Principal Amunition Technical Officer
PAU	Pilotless Aircraft Unit
PAVG	Prince Albert's Volunteer Guards
PAVO	Prince Albert Victor's Own
PAVOC	Prince Albert Victor's Own Cavalry
Paymr	Paymaster
PBF	Patrol Boat, Fast
PBFG	Patrol Boat, Fast, Guided Weapon
PC	Patrol Car
	Paymaster Captain
	Pioneer Corps
	Post Commander
	Principal Chaplain
	Punjab Cavalry
PCC	Postal & Courier Communications
PCE	Patrol Craft, Escort
P/CEA 3	Probationary Control Electrical Artificer 3rd class
PCG	Plain Clothes Gratuity
PCO	Principal Control Officer
P Cr	Paymaster Commander
PCS	Permanent Cruiser Service
PCW	Princess Charlotte of Wales's
PD	Pharmacy Dispenser
	Plans Division
	Precision Device
PDC	Practice Depth Charge
PDE	Projectile Development Establishment
P Det	Port Detachment
PDM	Pulse Delay Mechanism
PDMS	Point-Defence Missile System
Pdr	Pounder
PDRC	Personnel Despatch & Reception Centre
PE	Plastic Explosive
P/EA(A) 3	Probationary Electrical Artificer (Air) 3rd class
Pem Yeo	Pembroke Yeomanry
PF	Path Finder
	Position Finder

	Proximity Fuse
PFF	Pathfinder Force
	Police Field Force
	Punjab Frontier Force
PFNTU	Pathfinder Navigation Training Unit
PFO	Physical Fitness Officer
P/G	Postagram
PGB	Patrol Gunboat
Pho	Photographer
PI	Photographic Interpreter
PIAT	Projector, Infantry, Anti-Tank
PIF	Punjab Irregular Force
PIFF	Punjab Irregular Frontier Force
PIR	Pacific Islands Regiment
	Photographic Interpretation Report
PIY	Pembroke Imperial Yeomanry
PJI	Parachute Jump Instructor
PL	Paymaster Lieutenant
Pl	Platoon
P/L	Plain Language
PLH	Punjab Light Horse
Pln	Platoon
Plt Off	Pilot Officer
PLUTO	Pipe Line Under The Ocean
PM	Parachute Mine
	Patternmaker
	Prize Money
	Provost Marshal
PMA	Probationary Medical Assistant
P/Maj	Pipe-Major
PMC	President of the Mess Committee
P/MEA	Probationary Marine Engineering Artificer
PMF	Permanent Military Force
PMO	Principal Medical Officer
Pmr	Paymaster
PMRAFNS	Princess Mary's Royal Air Force Nursing Service
PMUB	Presbyterian, Methodist & United Board
PN	Pakistan Navy
P/N	Phonogram
PNTO	Principal Naval Transport Officer
PO	Petty Officer
	Pilot Officer
	Potential Officer
POA	Petty Officer Airman
POACMN	Petty Officer Aircrewman
POAF	Petty Officer Air Fitter

79

POC	Post Office Corps
POCA	Petty Officer Caterer
POCEL	Petty Officer Control Electrician
POCK	Petty Officer Cook
P/OEA 3	Probationary Ordnance Electrical Artificer 3rd class
POEL(A)	Petty Officer Electrician (Air)
(AW)	(Air Weapon)
POL	Petrol, Oil & Lubricants
POM	Potential Officer Material
	Priority of Movements
POMA	Petty Officer Medical Assistant
POME	Principal Ordnance Mechanical Engineer
POMEM	Petty Officer Marine Engineering Mechanic
POOEL	Petty Officer Ordnance Electrician
POPT	Petty Officer Physical Trainer
POR	Personnel Occurrence Report
POREL(A)	Petty Officer Radio Electrician (Air)
POSA	Petty Officer Stores Accountant
POSTD	Petty Officer Steward
POW	Prisoner of War
POWO	Prince/Princess of Wales's Own
POWRENAF	Petty Officer Wren Air Fitter
POWRENCINE	Petty Officer Wren Cinema Operator
POWRENCK	Petty Officer Wren Cook
POWRENDHYG	Petty Officer Wren Dental Hygienist
POWRENDSA	Petty Officer Wren Dental Surgery Assistant
POWRENHAIR	Petty Officer Wren Hairdresser
POWRENMET	Petty Officer Wren Meteorological Observer
POWRENMT	Petty Officer Wren Motor Transport Driver
POWRENPHOT	Petty Officer Wren Photographer
POWRENQA	Petty Officer Wren Quarters Assistant
POWREN(R)	Petty Officer Wren (Radar)
POWRENREL	Petty Officer Wren Radio Electrician
POWRENRS	Petty Officer Wren Radio Supervisor (Morse)
(M)	
POWRENSA	Petty Officer Wren Stores Accountant
POWRENS(C)	Petty Officer Wren Stores Assistant (Clothes)
POWRENS(S)	Petty Officer Wren Stores Assistant (Stores)
POWRENS(V)	Petty Officer Wren Stores Assistant (Victualling)
POWRENSTD	Petty Officer Wren Steward
POWRENTEL	Petty Officer Wren Telephonist
POWRENTSA	Petty Officer Wren Training Support Assistant
POWRENWA	Petty Officer Wren Weapon Analyst
POWRENWTR	Petty Officer Wren Writer (General)
(G)	
POWRENWTR	Petty Officer Wren Writer (Pay)
(P)	

POWRENWW	Petty Officer Wren Welfare Worker
POWTR	Petty Officer Writer
PPA	Popski's Private Army
PPCLI	Princess Patricia's Canadian Light Infantry
PPI	Plan Position Indicator
PPM	Pistol Prize Money
PPR	Paid Pensioner Recruiter
PR	Photographic Reconnaissance
	Protectorate Regiment
PRA	Paymaster Rear-Admiral
PRC	Personnel Reception Centre
	Polish Resettlement Corps
PRDG	Princess Royal's Dragoon Guards
P/REA	Probationary Radio Electrical Artificer
PRO	Pay & Records Office
Proby	Probationary
Prt	Private
	Provost
PRTI	Physical & Recreational Training Instructor
PRU	Photographic Reconnaissance Unit
PRV & FC	Pakistan Remount Veterinary & Remount Corps
PS	Patrol Service
	Project Study
psc	passed staff college
PSD	Personal Services Department
PSI	Permanent Staff Instructor
	Person of Special Importance
PSL	Paymaster Sub-Lieutenant
PSO	Personnel Selection Officer
	Polaris Systems Officer
	Principal Scientific Officer
	Principal Staff Officer
PSSCC	Peter Symonds School Cadet Corps
PT	Patrol Torpedo-boat
	Physical Training
PTC	Primary Training Centre
PT & W	Physical Training & Welfare
Pte	Private
PTI	Physical Training Instructor
PTS	Parachute Training School
PU	Personnel, Utility
PUO	Placed Under Observation
	Pyrexia of Unknown Origin
PV	Paravane
PVR	Pontefract Volunteer Rifles
	Premature Voluntary Release

PW	Platoon Weapons
	Prisoner of War
	Royal Warrant for Pay & Promotion
PWD	Psychological Warfare Division
PWE	Political Warfare Executive
PWI	Platoon Weapons Instructor
PWO	Prince/Princess of Wales's Own
	Principal Warfare Officer
PWOR	Princess of Wales's Own Regiment
PWRIMC	Prince of Wales Royal Indian Military College
PWSS	Port War Signal Station
PWV	Prince of Wales's Volunteers (South Lancashire Regiment)
PWX	Prisoners of War Executive
PY	Pembroke Yeomanry
PYC	Pembroke Yeomanry Cavalry
Q	Quarters
QA	Quarters Armourer
	Quarters Assistant
QAIMNS	Queen Alexandra's Imperial Military Nursing Service
QAIMNSR	Queen Alexandra's Imperial Military Nursing Service Reserve
QAMFNS	Queen Alexandra's Military Family Nursing Service
QAOGR	Queen Alexandra's Own Gurkha Rifles
QARANC	Queen Alexandra's Royal Army Nursing Corps
QARNNS	Queen Alexandra's Royal Naval Nursing Service
QARNNSR	Queen Alexandra's Royal Naval Nursing Service Reserve
QB	Queen's Bays
QCCB	Queen's College Cadet Battalion [Taunton]
QD	Quarterdeck
QDD	Qualified for Deep Diving
QDG	Queen's Dragoon Guards
QEO	Queen Elizabeth's Own
QER	Queen's Edinburgh Rifles
QF	Quick-Firing
QG	Qualified in Gunnery
QGE	Queen's Gurkha Engineers
QGM	Queen's Gallantry Medal
QGO	Queen's Gurkha Officer
QHM	Queen's Harbour Master
QI	Qualified Instructor
QIB	Queensland Imperial Bushmen
QL	Queen's Lancers
QLD	Queen's Light Dragoons
QLR	Queen's Lancashire Regiment

QM	Quartermaster
QMAAC	Queen Mary's Army Auxiliary Corps
QMCM	Quartermaster Corporal-Major
QMG	Quartermaster-General
QMGF	Quartermaster-General to the Forces
QMO	Queen Mary's Own
QMR	Queen Mary's Regiment
QMS	Quartermaster-Sergeant
QMSCC	Queen Mary's School Cadet Corps
QM Segt	Quartermaster-Sergeant
QMSI	Quartermaster-Sergeant Instructor
QMY	Queen Mary's Yeomanry
QO	Qualified in Ordnance
	Quarters Officer
	Queen's Own
QOCG	Queen's Own Corps of Guides
QOCH	Queen's Own Cameron Highlanders
QOD & WSY	Queen's Own Dorset & West Somerset Yeomanry
QODY	Queen's Own Dorsetshire Yeomanry
QOH	Queen's Own Hussars
QOLY	Queen's Own Lowland Yeomanry
QOMY	Queen's Own Mercian Yeomanry
QONR	Queen's Own Nigeria Regiment
QOOH	Queen's Own Oxfordshire Hussars
QOR	Queen's Own Rifles
QORGIY	Queen's Own Royal Glasgow Imperial Yeomanry
QORGY	Queen's Own Royal Glasgow Yeomanry
QOR of C	Queen's Own Rifles of Canada
QORR	Queen's Own Royal Regiment
QOWRK	Queen's Own Royal West Kent
QOWH	Queen's Own Worcestershire Hussars
QOY	Queen's Own Yeomanry
QR	Quarters Rating
	Queen's Rangers
	Queen's Regulations
QR & AI	Queen's Regulations and Admiralty Instructions
QRF	Quick Reaction Force
QRIH	Queen's Royal Irish Hussars
QRMF	Quick-Reacting Mobile Force
Qr Mr	Quartermaster
QRR	Queen's Royal Rifles
QRV	Queenstown Rifle Volunteers
QRVB	Queen's Rifle Volunteer Brigade
QSA	Qualified in Small Arms
QTO	Qualified Testing Officer
QUH	Queen's University Highland Battalion

QVO	Queen Victoria's Own
QVR	Queen Victoria's Rifles
QVS	Queen Victoria's School
QWAM	Qualified for Warrant Air Mechanic
QWE	Qualified for Warrant Engineer
QWM	Qualified for Warrant Mechanician
QWR	Queen's Westminster Rifles
QWRV	Queen's Westminster Rifle Volunteers
R	Radar
	Radiographer
	Range-taker
	Regiment
	Reserve
	Rifles
	Rigger
	Royal
	Run
R 1 DIY	Royal 1st Devon Imperial Yeomanry
RA	Range Assessor
	Ration Allowance
	Rear-Admiral
	Royal Regiment of Artillery
RAA	Royal Regiment of Australian Artillery
RA(A)	Rear-Admiral of Aircraft Carriers
RAABF	Royal Artillery Association Benevolent Fund
RAAC	Rhodesian Air Askari Corps
	Royal Australian Armoured Corps
RAADC	Royal Australian Army Dental Corps
RAAF	Royal Australian Air Force
RAAFNS	Royal Australian Air Force Nursing Service
RAAMC	Royal Australian Army Medical Corps
RAANC	Royal Australian Army Nursing Corps
RAAOC	Royal Australian Army Ordnance Corps
RAAPC	Royal Australian Army Pay Corps
RAASC	Royal Australian Army Service Corps
RAC	Royal Armoured Corps
	Royal Artillery Committee
RACD	Royal Army Clothing Department
RAChD	Royal Army Chaplains Department
RACS	Royal Australian Corps of Signals
RACT	Royal Australian Corps of Transport
RA(D)	Rear-Admiral of Destroyers
RADAR	Radio Detection And Ranging
RADC	Royal Army Dental Corps
RAE	Royal Aircraft Establishment

	Royal Australian Engineers
RA(E)	Engineer Rear-Admiral
RAEC	Royal Army Educational Corps
RAEME	Royal Australian Electrical & Mechanical Engineers
RAF	Royal Aircraft Factory
	Royal Air Force
RAFA	Royal Air Force Association
	Royal Australian Field Artillery
RAFBF	Royal Air Force Benevolent Fund
RAFC	Royal Artillery Flying Club
RAFCC	Royal Air Force Cinema Corporation
RAFES	Royal Air Force Educational Service
RAFFC	Royal Air Force Ferry Command
RAFG	Royal Air Force Germany
RAFME	Royal Air Force Middle East
RAFNS	Royal Air Force Nursing Service
RAFO	Reserve of Air Force Officers
RAFR	Royal Air Force Regiment
RAFSAA	Royal Air Force Small Arms Association
RAFSC	Royal Air Force Staff College
RAFSP	Royal Air Force Service Police
RAFTC	Royal Air Force Transport Command
RAFVR	Royal Air Force Volunteer Reserve
RAGA	Royal Australian Garrison Artillery
RAI	Royal Artillery Institution
RAIC	Royal Australian Infantry Corps
RAMC	Royal Army Medical Corps
RAN	Royal Australian Navy
RANAS	Rear-Admiral, Naval Air Stations
RANC	Royal Australian Naval College
RANFR	Royal Australian Naval Fleet Reserve
RANNS	Royal Australian Naval Nursing Service
RANR	Royal Australian Naval Reserve
RANVR	Royal Australian Naval Volunteer Reserve
RAO	Regimental Amalgamation Officer
RAOC	Royal Army Ordnance Corps
RAOC(E)	Royal Army Ordnance Corps (Engineering)
RAP	Regimental Aid Post
	Rocket-Assisted Projectile
RAPC	Royal Army Pay Corps
RAPWI	Repatriation of Allied Prisoners of War and Internees
RAR	Regular Army Reserve
	Rhodesian African Rifles
	Royal Australian Regiment
RARDEN	Royal Armament Research & Development Establishment Enfield

RARO	Regular Army Reserve of Officers
RAS	Replenishment At Sea
RASC	Royal Army Service Corps
RAT	Rocket-Assisted Torpedo
RATC	Rhodesian Air Training Centre
RATF	Radio Aids Training Flight
RATG	Rhodesian Air Training Group
R Aux AF	Royal Auxiliary Air Force
RAVC	Royal Army Veterinary Corps
RB	Rifle Brigade
RBH	Royal Bucks Hussars
RBL	Rifled Breech-Loader
	Royal British Legion
RBY	Royal Bucks Yeomanry
RBYC	Royal Berkshire Yeomanry Cavalry
RC	Regiment of Cavalry
R/C	Radio Control
RCA	Ration Cash Allowance
	Royal Canadian Artillery
RCAC	Royal Canadian Armoured Corps
RCAF	Royal Canadian Air Force
RCAMC	Royal Canadian Army Medical Corps
RCAPC	Royal Canadian Army Pay Corps
RCASC	Royal Canadian Army Service Corps
RCB	Regular Commissions Board
RCC	Rescue Co-ordination Centre
RC Ch	Roman Catholic Chaplain
RCCS	Royal Canadian Corps of Signals
RCD	Royal Canadian Dragoons
RCDC	Royal Canadian Dental Corps
RCDS	Royal College of Defence Studies
RCE	Railway Construction Engineer
	Corps of Royal Canadian Engineers
RCEME	Royal Canadian Electrical & Mechanical Engineers
RCF	Royal Carmarthen Fusiliers
RCHA	Royal Canadian Horse Artillery
RCL	Ramp Cargo Lighter
	Recoilless
RCM	Radar Counter-Measures
	Radio Counter-Measures
	Regimental Corporal-Major
	Regimental Court-Martial
RCN	Royal Canadian Navy
RCNC	Royal Corps of Naval Constructors
RCNR	Royal Canadian Naval Reserve
RCNVR	Royal Canadian Naval Volunteer Reserve

RCOC	Royal Canadian Ordnance Corps
RCP	Reflector-cum-Periscope
RCPC	Royal Canadian Postal Corps
RCR	Royal Canadian Regiment
RCS	Royal Corps of Signals
RCT	Regimental Combat Team
	Royal Corps of Transport
Rct	Recruit
RD	Royal Dragoons
	Royal Naval Reserve Decoration
R & D	Research & Development
RDC	Royal Defence Corps
RDF	Radio Direction-Finding
	Royal Dublin Fusiliers
RDH	Royal Deccan Horse
RDL	Rear Defence Locality
RDLI	Royal Durban Light Infantry
RDY	Royal Devon Yeomanry
RDYA	Royal Devon Yeomanry Artillery
RE	Radio Electrician
	Reconnaissance Experimental
	Corps of Royal Engineers
REA	Radio Electrical Artificer
REAN	Royal East African Navy
REBS	Royal Engineers Balloon School
Rec	Recruiter
Recce	Reconnaissance
RED	Radio Equipment Department
	Repairable Equipment Depot
REDS	Royal Engineers Diving School
REGPOWREN	Regulating Petty Officer Wren
Regt	Regiment
REKY	Royal East Kent Yeomanry
REL	Radio Electrician
REM	Radio Electrical Mechanic
REME	Corps of Royal Electrical & Mechanical Engineers
REMN	Radio Electrical Mechanician
REPS	Royal Engineers Postal Section
RERO	Royal Engineers Reserve of Officers
RF	Rapid Fire
	Reserve Flight
	Royal [Windsor] Foresters
	Royal Fusiliers
R & F	Rank & File
RFA	Royal Field Artillery
	Royal Fleet Auxiliary

RFC	Royal Flying Corps
RFEA	Regular Forces Employment Association
RFF	Royal Filling Factory
RFG	Rifle Fine Grain
Rfn	Rifleman
RFR	Royal Fleet Reserve
RG	Ranging Gun
R/G	Rear Gunner
RGA	Royal Garrison Artillery
	Royal Guernsey Artillery
RGF	Royal Gun Factory
RGG	Royal Grenadier Guards
RGH	Royal Gloucestershire Hussars
RGJ	Royal Green Jackets
RGPF	Royal Gunpowder Factory
RGR	Royal Garrison Regiment
	Royal Gurkha Regiment
Rgt	Regiment
RH	Railhead
	1st Nottinghamshire (Robin Hood) Rifle Volunteer Corps
	Royal Highlanders
	Royal Hospital, Chelsea
	Royal Hussars
RHA	Royal Horse Artillery
RHC	Royal Highlanders of Canada
RHF	Royal Highland Fusiliers
RHG	Royal Horse Guards
RHG1D	Royal Horse Guards & 1st Dragoons
RHLI	Royal Hamilton Light Infantry
RHMS	Royal Hibernian Military School
RHQ	Regimental Headquarters
RHR	Royal Highland Regiment
RHSC	Richmond Hill School Company
RI	Regimental Institute
	Rigorous Imprisonment
	Royal Irish [Regiment]
RIA	Royal Irish Artillery
RIAF	Royal Indian Air Force
RIASC	Royal Indian Army Service Corps
RID	Royal Irish Dragoons
RIDG	Royal Irish Dragoon Guards
RIF	Royal Irish Fusiliers
RIN	Royal Indian Navy
RINR	Royal Indian Naval Reserve
RINVR	Royal Indian Naval Volunteer Reserve
RIR	Regimental Inquiry Regulations

	Royal Irish Rifles
RIrF	Royal Irish Fusiliers
Ris	Risaldar
RIW	Repaired In Works
RJA	Royal Jersey Artillery
RJLI	Royal Jersey Light Infantry
RJM	Royal Jersey Militia
RL	Rocket Launcher
	Royal Lancers
RLG	Relief Landing Ground
	Rifle Large Grain
RLI	Rand Light Infantry
RLM	Royal Lancashire Militia
RLT	Regimental Landing Team
	Rolling Liquid Transporter
RM	Riding Master
	Royal Marines
RMA	Rear Maintenance Area
	Royal Malta Artillery
	Royal Marine Artillery
	Royal Marines Association
	Royal Military Academy
	Royal Military Asylum
RMAB	Royal Marines Auxiliary Brigade
RMAS	Royal Military Academy Sandhurst
RMAT	Royal Marine Advisory Team
RMB	Royal Marine Bands
RMBPD	Royal Marine Boom Patrol Detachment
RMC	Royal Military College
RMCC	Royal Military College of Canada
RMCS	Royal Military College of Science
RME	Royal Marine Engineers
RMF	Royal Munster Fusiliers
RMFA	Royal Malta Fencible Artillery
RMFVR	Royal Marine Forces Volunteer Reserve
RMG	Ranging Machine Gun
	Recommended for Medal & Gratuity
	Royal Marine Gunner
RML	Rescue Motor Launch
	Rifled Muzzle-Loader
RMLC	Royal Marine Labour Corps
RMLI	Royal Marine Light Infantry
RMMDBO	Royal Marine Mobile Defended Base Organization
RMNS	Royal Malayan Navy Ship
RMO	Regimental Medical Officer
	Royal Marine Office

RM Obs	Royal Marine Observer
R MON RE(M)	Royal Monmouthshire Royal Engineers (Militia)
RMP	Royal Marine Police
	Corps of Royal Military Police
RMR	Royal Malayan Regiment
	Royal Marine Reserve
	Royal Montreal Regiment
RMRA	Royal Marines Rifle Association
RMRO	Royal Marine Routine Orders
RMS	Royal Marine Signaller
RMSI	Royal Marine Signalling Instructor
RMSM	Royal Military School of Music
RMT	Reserve Mechanical Transport
RN	Royal Navy
RNA	Radio Navigational Aid
	Royal Naval Association
RNAD	Royal Naval Armament Depot
RNAEC	Rhodesia & Nyasaland Army Educational Corps
RNAF	Royal Naval Air Force
RNAH	Royal Naval Auxiliary Hospital
RNAS	Royal Naval Air Service
	Royal Naval Air Station
RNASBR	Royal Naval Auxiliary Sick Berth Reserve
RNAV	Royal Naval Artillery Volunteers
RNAW	Royal Naval Aircraft Workshop
RNAY	Royal Naval Aircraft Yard
RNB	Royal Naval Barracks
RNBD	Royal North British Dragoons
RNBF	Royal North British Fusiliers
RNBT	Royal Naval Benevolent Trust
RNC	Royal Naval College
RNCV	Royal Navy Coast Volunteers
RND	Royal Naval Division
RNDH	Royal North Devon Hussars
RNEC	Royal Naval Engineering College
RNF	Royal Northumberland Fusiliers
RNFC	Royal Naval Film Corporation
RNGM	Royal North Gloucestershire Militia
RNH	Royal Naval Hospital
RNMBR	Royal Naval Motor Boat Reserve
RNMS	Royal Naval Minewatching Service
RNO	Resident Naval Officer
RNPS	Royal Naval Patrol Service
RNR	Royal Naval Reserve
RNRA	Royal Naval Rifle Association
RNR(T)	Royal Naval Reserve (Trawlers)

RNSA	Royal Naval Sailing Association
RNSC	Royal Naval Staff College
RNSD	Royal Naval Stores Depot
RNS of M	Royal Naval School of Music
RNSQ	Royal Naval Sick Quarters
RNSR	Royal Naval Special Reserve
	Royal Nova Scotia Regiment
RNSS	Royal Naval Scientific Service
RNSTS	Royal Naval Supply & Transport Service
RNTE	Royal Naval Training Establishment
RNTU	Royal Naval Training Unit
RNV	Royal Naval Volunteer Reserve
RNVR	Royal Naval Volunteer Reserve
RNVR(A)	Royal Naval Volunteer Reserve (Air)
RNVSR	Royal Naval Volunteer Supplementary Reserve
RNV(W)R	Royal Naval Volunteer (Wireless) Reserve
RNWAR	Royal Naval Wireless Auxiliary Reserve
RNXS	Royal Naval Auxiliary Service
RNZA	Royal Regiment of New Zealand Artillery
RNZAC	Royal New Zealand Armoured Corps
RNZAEC	Royal New Zealand Army Educational Corps
RNZAF	Royal New Zealand Air Force
RNZAMC	Royal New Zealand Army Medical Corps
RNZAOC	Royal New Zealand Army Ordnance Corps
RNZASC	Royal New Zealand Army Service Corps
RNZChD	Royal New Zealand Chaplains Department
RNZCS	Royal New Zealand Corps of Signals
RNZDC	Royal New Zealand Dental Corps
RNZE	Corps of Royal New Zealand Engineers
RNZEME	Corps of Royal New Zealand Electrical & Mechanical Engineers
RNZIR	Royal New Zealand Infantry Regiment
RNZN	Royal New Zealand Navy
RNZNC	Royal New Zealand Nursing Corps
RNZNVR	Royal New Zealand Naval Volunteer Reserve
RNZPC	Royal New Zealand Pay Corps
RO	Observer (Radio)
	Radio Operator
	Regimental Orders
	Retired Officer
	Routine Order
RO1(G)	Radio Operator (General) 1st class
2	2nd class
RO1(W)	Radio Operator (Warfare) 1st class
2	2nd class
ROA	Reserve Officers' Association

ROC	Royal Observer Corps
ROD	Railway Operating Department
ROF	Royal Ordnance Factory
ROO	Railhead Ordnance Officer
ROP	Rate of Pay
ROTP	Regular Officer Training Programme
RP	Radar Plot
	Regimental Paymaster
	Regimental Police
	Reporting Post
	Restriction of Privileges
	Royal Provincials
RPA	Royal Pakistan Artillery
RPASC	Royal Pakistan Army Service Corps
RPC	Remount Purchasing Commission
	Royal Pioneer Corps
RPE	Royal Pakistan Engineers
RPG	Rounds per Gun
RPH	Remotely Piloted Helicopter
RPL	Ramped Powered Lighter
RPM	Rifle Prize Money
	Rounds per Minute
RPN	Royal Pakistan Navy
RPNVR	Royal Pakistan Naval Volunteer Reserve
RPO	Regulating Petty Officer
RPR	Railway Pioneer Regiment
RPV	Remote Piloted Vehicle
RQMC	Regimental Quartermaster-Corporal
RQMS	Regimental Quartermaster-Sergeant
RR	Rand Rifles
	Recommended for Re-engagement
	Reserve Regiment
	Rhodesia Regiment
	Rough Riders (City of London Yeomanry)
R & R	Rest & Recuperation
RRAF	Royal Rhodesian Air Force
RRC	Rigid Raiding Craft
RRF	Royal Regiment of Fusiliers
RRR	Royal Rhodesia Regiment
RRSM	Rough Riding Sergeant-Major
RRSSM	Rough Riding Staff Sergeant-Major
RRW	Royal Regiment of Wales
RS	Royal Scots
RSAF	Royal Small Arms Factory
RSB	Regimental Stretcher-Bearer
RSDG	Royal Scots Dragoon Guards

RSF	Royal Scots Fusiliers
RSG	Royal Scots Greys
R SIGS	Royal Corps of Signals
RSL	Returned Servicemen's League
RSM	Regimental Sergeant-Major
	Royal Surrey Militia
RS & M	Royal Sappers & Miners
RSME	Royal School of Military Engineering
RSR	Raiding Support Regiment
RSRE	Royal Signals & Radar Establishment
RSRM	Raiding Squadron Royal Marines
RS(S)	Radio Supervisor (Special)
RSSAILA	Returned Sailors', Soldiers', Airmen's Imperial League of Australia
RSU	Repair & Salvage Unit
RS(W)	Radio Supervisor (Warfare)
RSWD	Regiment South Western District
RT	Rangetaker
R/T	Radio-Telephony
RTB	Return To Base
RTC	Royal Tank Corps
RTE	Railway Transport Establishment
RTO	Railway Transport Officer
RTR	Le Regiment de Trois-Rivieres
	Royal Tank Regiment
RTT	Radio Teletype
RTU	Returned To Unit
RTW	Railway Tank Wagon
RU	Reinforcement Unit
RUR	Royal Ulster Rifles
RUSI	Royal United Service Institution
	Royal United Services Institute for Defence Studies
RUSM	Royal United Service Museum
RV	Rendezvous
	Rifle Volunteers
RVB	Royal Veteran Battalion
RVC	Rifle Volunteer Corps
RVH	Reserve Veterinary Hospital
RVTC	Rochester Volunteer Training Corps
RW	Royal Warrant
RWAFF	Royal West African Frontier Force
RWARF	Royal Warwickshire Fusiliers
R War R	Royal Warwickshire Regiment
RWE	Radio Warfare Establishment
RWF	Royal Welch Fusiliers
	Royal Welsh Fusiliers

RWIY	Royal Wiltshire Imperial Yeomanry
RWK	Queen's Own Royal West Kent Regiment
RWP	Regiment Western Province
RWS	Royal West Surrey Regiment
RWY	Royal Wiltshire Yeomanry
RY	Royal Yeomanry
RYR	Royal Yeomanry Regiment
S	Seaman
	Sepoy
	Signaller
	Sniper
	Sonar
	Stores
	Surveyor
SA	Semi-Automatic
	Servant Allowance
	Small Arms
	Stores Accountant
	Stores Assistant
	Supply Accountant
	Sweep, Acoustic
SA 111 VC	3rd Sussex Artillery Volunteer Corps
SAA	Small Arms Ammunition
	South Australian Artillery
SAAD	Small Arms Ammunition Depot
SAAF	South African Air Force
SAAPCC	South African Administrative Pay & Clerical Corps
SAARF	Special Allied Airborne Reconnaissance Force
SAC	Senior Aircraftman
	School of Army Co-operation
SACEUR	Supreme Allied Commander Europe
SACLANT	Supreme Allied Commander Atlantic
SACMP	South African Corps of Military Police
SACS	South African Corps of Signals
SACSEA	Supreme Allied Commander South East Asia
SACW	Senior Aircraftwoman
SADE	Specialized Armoured Development Establishment.
SADF	South African Defence Force
SAE	Specialized Armoured Establishment
SAEC	South African Engineers Corps
SAF	School of Aerial Fighting
SAGW	Surface-to-Air Guided Weapon
SALH	South Alberta Light Horse
SAM	Surface-to-Air Missile
SAMC	South African Medical Corps

SA & MGS	Small Arms & Machine Gun School
SAMR	South African Mounted Rifles
SANF	South African Naval Forces
SANLC	South African Native Labour Corps
SANS	South African Naval Service
SAO	Senior Administrative Officer
SAOC	South African Ordnance Corps
SAP	Semi-Armour Piercing
SAPI	Semi-Armour Piercing, Incendiary
SAR	Search And Rescue
SARAH	Search And Rescue And Homing
SAS	Small Arms School
	Special Air Service
SASC	Small Arms School Corps
SASO	Senior Air Staff Officer
	Superintending Armament Supply Officer
SATC	South African Tank Corps
SATS	Small Arms Target System
	South African Training Ship
SAU	Surface Attack Unit
SAVC	South African Veterinary Corps
SAWANS	South African Women's Auxiliary Naval Service
SB	Sam Browne
	Signal Boatswain
	Small Bore
	Smooth Bore
	Stretcher Bearer
SBA	Sick Berth Attendant
SBC	Sam Browne's Cavalry
SBCPO	Sick Bay Chief Petty Officer
SBF	Standby Flying
SBML	Smooth Bore Muzzle Loading
SBNO	Senior British Naval Officer
SBR	Small Box-Respirator
SBS	Special Boat Section
SB Sqn	Special Boat Squadron
SBT	Submarine Bubble Target
SC	Scrap Carriage
	Service Certificate
	Southern Command
	Staff Captain
	Staff Corps
	Strike Command
	Suffolk & Cambridgeshire Regiment
	Swimmer-Canoeist
S/C	Submarine Coxswain

95

SCA	Soldiers Christian Association
SCAEF	Supreme Commander Allied Expeditionary Force
SCC	Sea Cadet Corps
	Senior Command Course
SCEA	Service Children's Education Authority
SCF	Senior Chaplain to the Forces
SCGM	Senior Cook General Mess
SCI	Smoke Curtain Installation
	Ship-Controlled Interception
SCLI	Somerset & Cornwall Light Infantry
SCMR	South Canterbury Mounted Rifles
SCNO	Senior Canadian Naval Officer
SCPL	Staff of Chief of Personnel & Logistics
SCM	Squadron Corporal-Major
	Summary Court-Martial
SCO	Senior Chief Officer
SCOH	Staff Corporal of Horse
S/Corp	Staff Corporal
SCOSE	Standing Committee On Submarine Escape
S/Cpl	Staff Corporal
SCRDE	Stores & Clothing Research & Development Establishment
SD	Service Dress
	Signals Division
	Special Duties
	Staff Duties
	Stores Depot
	Submarine Detector
	Supply Detachment
SDB	Seaward Defence Boat
SDC	Seaward Defence Craft
SDF	Sudan Defence Force
SDG	Stormont, Dundas & Glengarry Highlanders
SDI	Submarine Detector Instructor
SDO	Signal Distribution Officer
SD & T	Staff Duties & Training
SE	Safety Equipment
	Santos Dumont Experimental
	Scouting Experimental
S/E	Single-Engined
SEAAC	South East Asia Air Command
SEAC	South East Asia Command
SEADEX	Seaward Defence Exercise
SEALF	South-East Asia Land Forces
SEATO	South-East Asia Treaty Organization
SEB	Special Engagement Bonus

Sec	Section
	Sector
SEE	Signals Experimental Establishment
SEL	School of Electric Light
	Semi-Effective List
Sen	Senior
Serg	Sergeant
Sergt	Sergeant
Serj	Serjeant
Serjt	Serjeant
SESO	Senior Equipment Staff Officer
SETC	Submarine Escape Training Centre
SF	Royal Scots Fusiliers
	Servicing Flight
SFO	Senior Flag Officer
SFTS	Service Flying Training School
SG	Scots Greys
	Scots Guards
	Seaman Gunner
	Royal South Gloucestershire Light Infantry Militia
Sg	Surgeon
SGB	Steam Gunboat
Sg C	Surgeon Captain
Sg Cr	Surgeon Commander
Sg L Cr	Surgeon Lieutenant-Commander
Sg R A	Surgeon Rear-Admiral
Sgt	Sergeant
Sgt-Maj	Sergeant-Major
SGU	Single Gun Unit
Sg VA	Surgeon Vice-Admiral
SH	Scinde Horse
	Scottish Horse
	Southland Hussars
Sh	Shipwright
SHAEF	Supreme Headquarters Allied Expeditionary Force
SHAPE	Supreme Headquarters Allied Powers in Europe
SHD	Ship's Diver
SHG	Shorthand Typist (Higher Grade)
SHQ	Squadron Headquarters
	Station Headquarters
Sh L	Shipwright Lieutenant
SI	Sergeant Instructor
SIB	Special Investigation Branch
Sig	Signal
Sig L	Signal Lieutenant
Sig O	Signal Officer

SIH	Scinde Irregular Horse
	South Irish Horse
SINS	Ships Inertial Navigation System
SIO	Senior Intelligence Officer
SIS	Special Intelligence Service
SITREP	Situation Report
SIU	Special Investigation Unit
SIW	Self-Inflicted Wound
SIY	Shropshire Imperial Yeomanry
	South of Ireland Yeomanry
	Staffordshire Imperial Yeomanry
	Sussex Imperial Yeomanry
Sjt	Serjeant
S/KA	Submarine Kit Allowance
SKC	Services Kinema Corporation
SKD	Station Keeping Distance
Skr	Skipper
SL	Searchlight
	Squadron Leader
	Sub-Lieutenant
SLAM	Supersonic Low Altitude Missile
	Surface-Launched Air Missile
SLBM	Sea-Launched Ballistic Missile
	Submarine-Launched Ballistic Missile
SLC	Searchlight Control
SLD	Sea Landing Division
S/Ldr	Squadron Leader
SLG	Satellite Landing Ground
	Shorthand Typist (Lower Grade)
SLI	Sikh Local Infantry
	Shropshire Light Infantry
	Somerset Light Infantry
SLM	Surrey Local Militia
SLMD(RA)	Searchlight Militia Depot (Royal Artillery)
Slmr	Sailmaker
SLMSC	South London (Volunteers) Medical Staff Corps
SLO	Searchlight Operator
SLR	Self-Loading Rifle
	Sierra Leone Regiment
SLRA	Sierra Leone Royal Artillery
SLRV	South London Regiment of Volunteers
S Lt	Sub-Lieutenant
SLU	Special Liaison Unit
SM	Seamen
	Sergeant-Major
	Submarine

	Submarine Miners
S & M	Sappers & Miners
SMC	Sub-Machine Carbine
SME	School of Military Engineering
SMG	Sub-Machine Gun
SMGO	Senior Military Government Officer
SMI	Sergeant-Major Instructor
SMIG	Sergeant-Major Instructor of Gunnery
SMLE	Short Magazine Lee-Enfield
SMM	Submarine Miners
SMO	Senior Medical Officer
SMP	Self-Maintenance Period
SMPS	Special Mobile Provost Section
SMR	Saskatchewan Mounted Rifles
	Senior Maintenance Rating
SMRV	South Middlesex Rifle Volunteers
SMTO	Senior Mechanical Transport Officer
SNCO	Senior Non-Commissioned Officer
SNH	South Nottinghamshire Hussars
SNLR	Services No Longer Required
SNO	Senior Naval Officer
SNOPG	Senior Naval Officer Persian Gulf
SNOWI	Senior Naval Officer West Indies
SNS	Senior Nursing Sister
SNSO	Superintending Naval Stores Officer
SNYC	South Nottinghamshire Yeomanry Cavalry
SO	Section Officer
	Senior Officer
	Special Operations
	Staff Officer
	Stores Officer
S(O)	Seaman (Operator)
SOA	Staff Officer, Administration
SOAD	Staff Officer, Air Defence
SOC	Struck Off Charge
SOE	Senior Officer Escort
	Special Operations Executive
S of A	School of Artillery
S of G	School of Gunnery
S of I	School of Infantry
	Superintendent of Instruction
S of M	School of Musketry
SO-in-C	Signal Officer-in-Chief
SOME	Senior Ordnance Mechanical Engineer
SOMS	Senior Officer Minesweepers
SONAR	Sonic Azimuth and Ranging

SOO	Staff Operations Officer
SO(O)	Staff Officer (Operations)
SOP	Staff Officer of Pensioners
	Standard Operating Procedure
SOS	Struck Off Strength
SO & S	Scouting, Observation & Sniping
SOWC	Senior Officers War Course
SP	Self-Propelled
	Service Police
	Signalling Projector
	Signal Publication
	Smokeless Propellant
	Sniper's Post
	Special Proficiency
	Staff Paymaster
	Starting Point
	Station Police
S/P	Submarine Pay
SPDC	Spare Parts Distributing Centre
SPG	Self-Propelled Gun
SPL	Self-Propelled Launcher
SPMR	Southern Provinces Mounted Rifles
SPP	Special Proficiency Pay
Spr	Sapper
SPRO	Services Public Relations Officer
SPRR	Self-Propelled Recoilless Rifle
SPSO	Senior Personnel Selection Officer
SPTI	Senior Physical Training Instructor
SQ	Sick Quarters
	Specialist Qualifications
Sqdn	Squadron
Sqdn Ldr	Squadron-Leader
SQMC	Squadron Quartermaster-Corporal
SQMS	Squadron Quartermaster-Sergeant
	Staff Quartermaster-Sergeant
Sqn	Squadron
Sqn Ldr	Squadron-Leader
Sq O	Squadron Officer
Sqn Obs	Squadron Observer
Sqn Offr	Squadron Officer
SQO	Senior Quarters Officer
SR	Scottish Rifles
	Service Rifle
	Simla Rifles
	Special Reserve
	Submarine Recorder

	Supplementary Reserve
	Surveyor
	Survey Recorder
SRA	Southern Rhodesia Artillery
	Surgeon Rear-Admiral
SRACR	Southern Rhodesia Armoured Car Regiment
SRAFO	Senior Royal Air Force Officer
SRBM	Short Range Ballistic Missile
SRCMP	Southern Rhodesia Corps of Military Police
SRD	Service Rum Diluted
SRDE	Signals Research & Development Establishment
SRE	Sound Reproduction Equipment
SRE(V)	Singapore Royal Engineers (Volunteers)
SRGSC	Southern Rhodesia General Service Corps
SRIY	Sherwood Rangers Imperial Yeomanry
SRP	Supply Refilling Point
SRTC	Southern Rhodesia Transport Corps
SRY	Sherwood Rangers Yeomanry
SS	Sea Service
	Sharpshooters (3rd County of London Yeomanry)
	Special Service
	Staff Surgeon
	Submarine Scout
	Superintending Sister
S/S	Single Seater
SSA	Star of South Africa
SSAFA	Soldiers', Sailors' & Airmen's Families Association
SSB	- Special Service Battalion
SSBN	Ships Submersible Ballistic Nuclear
SSD	Soldiers Service Dress
SSE	Submarine Scout Experimental
SSEF	Support Squadron Eastern Flank
SSF	Single-Seater Fighter
S/Sgt	Staff Sergeant
SSGW	Surface-to-Surface Guided Weapon
SSM	Squadron Sergeant-Major
	Staff Sergeant-Major
	Surface-to-Surface Missile
SSO	Senior Supply Officer
	Squadron Signals Officer
	Staff Signals Officer
	Station Staff Officer
SSOTC	Skinner's School Officers Training Corps
SSP	Submarine Scout Patrol
SSQ	Station Sick Quarters
SSRF	Small Scale Raiding Force

SSS	Shore Signal Service
SST	Submarine Scout Twin-type
SS/T	Supersonic Telegraphy
SSTO	Superintending Sea Transport Officer
SSVF	Straits Settlements Volunteer Force
SSW	Secretary of State for War
S & Sx Yeo	Surrey & Sussex Yeomanry
SSY	Sharpshooters Yeomanry
	South Somerset Yeomanry
ST	Seaman Torpedoman
	Shorthand Writer
	Stenographer
	Stick Type
S/T	Sonic Telegraphy
STAAG	Standard Tachymetric Anti-Aircraft Gun
STAA	Soldiers Total Abstinence Association
STANAVFOR-CHAN	Standing Naval Force, Channel
STANAVFOR-LANT	Standing Naval Force, Atlantic
STC	Senior Training Corps
	SHAPE Technical Centre
	Signal Training Centre
S & T Corps	Supply & Transport Corps
STD	Sea Transport Department
	Steward
Stn	Station
STO	Sea Transport Officer
STOL	Short Take-Off & Landing
STRE	Specialist Team Royal Engineers
STSO	Senior Technical Staff Officer
STT	School of Tank Technology
	School of Technical Training
STU	Special Training Unit
SU	Signals Unit
	Supply
Sub	Subedar
SUBACLANT	Submarine Allied Command, Atlantic
Sub-Lt	Sub-Lieutenant
SUBROC	Submarine-launched Rocket
SUE	Signal Underwater Exploding
SUIT	Sight Unit Infantry Trilux
SUM	Surface-to-Underwater Missile
SUO	Senior Under-Officer
Supt	Superintendent
SUSM	Scottish United Services Museum

SV	Support Vehicle
SVA	Singapore Volunteer Artillery
SVAC	Singapore Volunteer Artillery Corps
SVC	Shangai Volunteer Corps
	Singapore Volunteer Corps
SVI	Singapore Volunteer Infantry
SVLH	Surma Valley Light Horse
SVO	Senior Veterinary Officer
SVP	Services Vegetable Production
SVR	Singapore Volunteer Rifles
SVSO	Superintending Victualling Stores Officer
SVTC	Surrey Volunteer Training Corps
SW	Shallow Water Diver
SWB	South Wales Borderers
SWD	Special Water Dispenser
SWH	Scottish Women's Hospital
SWO	Senior Warrant Officer
	Squadron Wireless Officer
	Station Warrant Officer
SWOP	Switchboard Operator
SWS	Shore Wireless Service
SY	Shropshire Yeomanry
	Sussex Yeomanry
SY & LI	Sherwood Yeomanry & Light Infantry
Sy PO	Supply Petty Officer
T	Telegraphist
	Temperance
	Territorial
	Tracker
	Tradesman
	Turner
TA	Territorial Army
	Training Allowance
	Trinidad Artillery
TAA	Territorial Army Association
TAAFA	Territorial Army & Air Force Association
Tac	Tactical
Tac R	Tactical Reconnaissance
TAF	Tactical Air Force
TAFA	Territorial & Auxiliary Forces Association
TAG	Telegraphist Air Gunner
TANS	Territorial Army Nursing Association
TAOR	Tactical Area Of Responsibility
TAR	Territorial Army Regulations
TARA	Technical Assistant Royal Artillery

	Territorial Army Rifle Association
TARE	Telegraphic Automatic Relay Equipment
TARO	Territorial Army Reserve of Officers
TAS	Torpedo & Anti-Submarine
	True Air Speed
TASI	Torpedo & Anti-Submarine Instructor
TASM	Tactical Air-to-Surface Missile
TASWD	Torpedo, Anti-Submarine & Mine Warfare Division
TAT	Temporary Ambulance Train
TAVR	Territorial & Army Volunteer Reserve
TB	Torpedo-Boat
	Training Battalion
T/B	Torpedo Bomber
TBD	Torpedo-Boat Destroyer
TBR	Torpedo Bomber Reconnaissance
TBS	Talk Between Ships
TC	Tactical Command
	Tank Corps
	Temporary Chaplain
	Torpedo Control
	Torpedo Coxswain
	Traffic Control
	Training Corps
	Transport Command
	Transvaal Cadets
	Troop Carrier
TCBG	Training Centre Brigade of Gurkhas
TCDU	Transport Command Development Unit
TCF	Temporary Chaplain to the Forces
	Territorial Cadet Force
TCM	Troop Corporal-Major
TCO	Tactical Control Officer
	Torpedo Control Officer
	Train Conducting Officer
TCP	Transport Command Police
TCU	Transport Conversion Unit
TCV	Troop Carrying Vehicle
TCW	Troop Carrier Wing
TD	Tank Destroyer
	Telegraphist Detector
	Territorial Decoration
	Trade Division
	Tyne Division
TDBG	Training Depot Brigade of Gurkhas
TDC	Through-Deck-Cruiser
TDF	Tonga Defence Force

TDI	Telegraphist Detector Instructor
TDS	Training Depot Station
TDT	Turret Director Trainer
TE	Tatin Experimental
	Training Establishment
T/E	Twin-Engined
Tech Adj	Technical Adjutant
TEU	Tropical Experimental Unit
TEV	Terminal Equipment Vehicle
TEWT	Tactical Exercise Without Troops
TF	Task Force
	Territorial Force
	Training Flight
	Flying Training
	Trench Fighter
TFA	Territorial Force Association
TFNS	Territorial Force Nursing Service
TFR	Territorial Force Reserve
TGM	Torpedo Gunner's Mate
TG or UA	Temperance, Grog or Underage
THA	Transvaal Horse Artillery
TI	Target Indicator
	Torpedo Instructor
TIB	Tasmanian Imperial Bushmen
TISC	Treasury Inter-Services Committee
TJFF	Trans-Jordan Frontier Force
TL	Torpedo Lieutenant
T/L	Telegraphist Lieutenant
TLI	Trinidad Light Infantry
TLS	Tank Laser Sight
TLW	Torpedo Lieutenant's Writer
TM	Town Major
	Trained Man
	Trench Mortar
TMB	Trench Mortar Battery
TMR	Transvaal Mounted Rifles
Tmr	Trimmer
TM/S	Trained in Minesweeping
Tng	Training
TO	Torpedo Officer
	Trained Operator
	Transport Officer
Toc H	Talbot House
TOCU	Tornado Operational Conversion Unit
TOD	Time of Despatch
TOL	Trucial Oman Levies

TOS	Trucial Oman Scouts
TOO	Time of Origin
TOS	Tactical Operations System
	Taken on Strength
TOW	Target on Wire
	Tube-Launched Optically-Tracked Wire-Command
Tp	Troop
TPM	Torpedo Prize Money
Tpr	Trooper
TQMS	Technical Quartermaster-Sergeant
	Troop Quartermaster-Sergeant
Tr	Troop
	Trumpeter
TR	Territorial Reserve
TRE	Telecommunications Research Establishment
Trg	Training
TRV	Torpedo Recovery Vehicle
TS	Trained Soldier
	Training Squadron
	Transmitting Station
	Tyneside Scottish
tsc	Territorial staff course
TSD	Tactical & Staff Duties
	Transportation Stores Depot
TSF	Two-Seater Fighter
TSM	Troop Sergeant-Major
TSMG	Thompson Submachine Gun
TSR	Tactical Strike Reconnaissance
	Torpedo Spotter Reconnaissance
TT	Target-Tower
	Telecommunications Technician
	Torpedo Tube
	Turret Trainer
	Tyne & Tees (50th Northumbrian Division)
TTC	Technical Training Centre
TTF	Target Towing Flight
TTTE	Tri-national Tornado Training Establishment
TURCO	Turn-Round Control Organisation
TV	Trinidad Volunteers
TVC	Tientsin Volunteer Corps
TVR	Tadcaster Volunteer Rifles
TWE	Trading With the Enemy
TWU	Tactical Weapons Unit
TY	Territorial Yeomanry
Ty	Temporary

UA	Under Age
UAM	Underwater-to-Air Missile
UAS	University Air Squadron
UC 1	Underwater Control Rating 1st class
2	2nd class
UCWRE	Underwater Counter-Measures & Weapons Research Establishment
UDF	Union Defence Force
UDR	Ulster Defence Regiment
UDT	Underwater Destruction Team
UDU	Underwater Destruction Unit
UE	Unit Establishment
UET	Unit Equipment Table
ufp	unemployed full pay
UJC	Union Jack Club
UKADGE	United Kingdom Air Defence Ground Environment
UKCICC	United Kingdom Commanders-in-Chief's Committee
UKJATFOR	United Kingdom Joint Airborne Task Force
UKLF	United Kingdom Land Forces
UKMF(A)	United Kingdom Mobile Force (Air)
UKMF(L)	United Kingdom Mobile Force (Land)
ULLA	Ultra-Low Level Air-drop
ULOTC	University of London Officer Training Corps
Un Bd Ch	United Board Chaplain
UNFICYP	United Nations Forces in Cyprus
UOTC	University Officers Training Corps
UP	Unrotated Projectile
UPS	Universities & Public Schools Battalion
UR	Uganda Rifles
U/S	Unserviceable
USC	United Services Club
USGW	Underwater-to-Surface Guided Weapon
usl	unemployed supernumerary list
USSF	Ulster Special Service Force
U/T	Under Training
UTC	University Training Corps
UTP	Upper Thames Patrol
UUM	Underwater-to-Underwater Missile
UVR	Uitenhage Volunteer Rifles
UW	Underwater Weapons
UWD	Underwater Weapons Department
UXAA	Unexploded Anti-Aircraft Shell
UXAPB	Unexploded Anti-Personnel Bomb
UXB	Unexploded Bomb
UXGB	Unexploded Gas Bomb
UXIB	Unexploded Incendiary Bomb

UXO	Unexploded Object
UXPM	Unexploded Parachute Mine
UXS	Unexploded Shell
UYC	Uxbridge Yeomanry Cavalry
V	Vergeltungswaffe (reprisal, or vengeance, weapon)
	V1 flying bomb
	V2 rocket
	V3 London gun
	Victualling
	Volunteers
VA	Vice-Admiral
	Victualling Allowance
	Vulnerable Area
VAD	Voluntary Aid Detachment
V Adm	Vice-Admiral
VAR	Corps of Volunteers Artillery Regiment
VAS	Veterinary Assistant Surgeon
VB	Volunteer Battalion
VBGH	Volunteer Battalion Gordon Highlanders
VC	Victoria Cross
VCAS	Vice-Chief of Air Staff
VCDS	Vice-Chief of Defence Staff
VCG	Calcutta Volunteer Guards
VCIGS	Vice-Chief of the Imperial General Staff
VCO	Viceroy's Commissioned Officer
VCNS	Vice-Chief of Naval Staff
VCOS	Vice-Chiefs of Staff
VCP	Vehicle Check Point
	Veterinary Collecting Post
VD	Royal Naval Volunteer Reserve Decoration
VDA	Variable Depth Asdic
VDC	Volunteer Defence Corps
VDG	5th Royal Inniskilling Dragoon Guards
VDMSC	Volunteer Durham Medical Staff Corps
VDS	Variable Depth Sonar
VEB	Variable Elevation Beam
VE Day	Victory Europe Day (8/5/45)
VES	Veterinary Evacuating Station
VGO	Vickers Gas Operated
VG	Volunteer Guards
VH	Veterinary Hospital
VIAC	Vienna Allied Command
VIB	Volunteer Infantry Brigade
VIP	Very Important Person
VJ Day	Victory Japan Day (15/8/45)

VLBTI	Very Long-Burning Target Indicator
VLR	Very Long Range
VM	Victory Medal
VMG	Vickers Machine Gun
VMR	Victoria Mounted Rifles
VO	Veterinary Officer
Vol	Volunteer
Volr	Volunteer
VP	Vulnerable Point
VR	Volunteer Regiment
	Volunteer Reserve
VRBG	Viceroy's Bodyguard
VRC	Victoria Rifles of Canada
	Volunteer Rifle Corps
VRCS	Veterinary & Remount Conducting Section
VRD	Vehicle Reception Depot
	Royal Naval Volunteer Reserve Decoration
VRM	Van Riebeeck Medal
VRS	Veterinary & Remount Service
VRT	Voluntary Reserve Training
V/S	Visual Signalling
VSA	Victualling Store Allowance
VSC	Volunteer Staff Corps
VSO	Victualling Stores Officer
V/STOL	Vertical/Short Take-Off & Landing
VT	Variable Time Fuse
VTC	Volunteer Training Corps
VTOL	Vertical Take-Off & Landing
VY	Victualling Yard
W	Writer
WA	Weapon Armourer
	Weapons Analyst
	Wedge Action
	Western Approaches
WAAAF	Women's Australian Auxiliary Air Force
WAAC	War Artists' Advisory Committee
	Women's Army Auxiliary Corps
	Women's Auxiliary Army Corps
WAAF	Women's Auxiliary Air Force
WAC	West Africa Command
WACI	Western Approaches Convoy Instructions
	Women's Army Corps of India
WAF	West African Forces
	Women's Auxiliary Force
WAFF	West African Frontier Force

WAFS	Women's Air Force Services
WAG	Wireless Air Gunner
WAGS	Wireless Air Gunners School
WANS	Women's Australian National Service
WAR	West African Regiment
WASPS	Women's Agricultural Security Production Service
WATS	Women's Auxiliary Territorial Service
WAWC	West Africa War Council
W & B	Works & Building Services
WBVRC	West Bromwich Volunteer Rifle Corps
WC	War Cabinet
W/C	White Clothing
W & C	Westmorland & Cumberland Yeomanry
W/Cdr	Wing-Commander
WCIY	Westmorland & Cumberland Imperial Yeomanry
WCO	Warrant Communication Officer
W Comm	Wing-Commander
WCYC	Westmorland & Cumberland Yeomanry Cavalry
WD	War Department
	Westminster Dragoons
WDAF	Western Desert Air Force
WDC	War Department Constabulary
WDF	Western Desert Force
W Dgns	Westminster Dragoons
Wdr	Wardmaster
WDRC	Women's Defence Relief Corps
Wdr L	Wardmaster Lieutenant
WDTU	War Dog Training Unit
WDU	Wireless Development Unit
WE	War Establishment
	Weapons Engineering
	Webbing Equipment
WEC	Women's Emergency Corps
WEO	Weapons Engineer Officer
WEOW	Weapons Engineer Officer's Writer
WF	Welch Fusiliers
WFC	Women's Forage Corps
WFF	Western Frontier Force
WFR	Worcestershire & Sherwood Foresters Regiment
WG	Welsh Guards
Wg Cdr	Wing-Commander
Wg Cndr	Wing-Commander
Wg Cr	Wing-Commander
Wg O	Wing Officer
Wg Offr	Wing Officer
WH	Welsh Horse

WIDU	Wireless Intelligence & Development Unit
WIR	War Information Report
	West Indian Regiment
WIRGA	West Indian Royal Garrison Artillery
WKIY	West Kent Imperial Yeomanry
Wksp	Workshop
WKVF	West Kent Volunteer Force
WKY	Warwickshire Yeomanry
	West Kent Yeomanry
WL	Women's Legion
WLA	Women's Land Army
WM	Warrant Mechanician
	Weapon Mechanician
WMAA	Warrant Master-at-Arms
WNLSC	Women's National Land Service Corps
WNSR	West Nova Scotia Regiment
WO	War Office
	Warrant Officer
	Welfare Officer
	Wireless Operator
	Writer Officer
	Written Off
WOCCI	War Office Central Card Index
WOCL	War Office Casualty List
WOL	War Office Letter
WOM	Wireless Operator Mechanic
WOMP	Western Ocean Meeting Point
WOO	Warrant Ordnance Officer
W/Op	Wireless Operator
WOSB	War Office Selection Board
WOSD	Weapons Operational Systems Development
WP	Weather Permitting
	White Phosphorus
	Wolseley Pattern
WPC	War Pensions Committee
WR	Ward Room
	War Reserve
WRA	Ward Room Attendant
WRAAF	Women's Royal Australian Air Force
WRAAC	Women's Royal Australian Army Corps
WRAC	Women s Royal Army Corps
WRAF	Women's Royal Air Force
WRAFVR	Women's Royal Air Force Volunteer Reserve
WRANS	Women's Royal Australian Naval Service
WRAS	Women's Reserve Ambulance Society
WRCNS	Women's Royal Canadian Naval Service

WRE	Weapons Research Establishment
WRENACK	Wren Assistant Cook
WRENAM	Wren Air Mechanic
WRENCINE (AB)	Wren Cinema Operator (Able)
WRENCINE (ORD)	Wren Cinema Operator (Ordinary)
WRENCK	Wren Cook
WRENDHYG	Wren Dental Hygienist
WRENDSA	Wren Dental Surgery Assistant
WRENEDUC	Wren Education Assistant
WRENHAIR	Wren Hairdresser
WRENMET	Wren Meteorological Observer
WRENMT	Wren Motor Transport Driver
WRENPHOT	Wren Photographer
WRENQ A	Wren Quarters Assistant
WREN(R)	Wren (Radar)
WRENREG	Wren Regulating
WRENREM	Wren Radio Electrical Mechanic
WRENRO(M)1	Wren Radio Operator (Morse) 1st class
2	2nd class
WRENSA	Wren Stores Accountant
WRENS(C)	Wren Stores Assistant (Clothes)
(S)	(Stores)
(V)	(Victualling)
WRENSTD	Wren Steward
WRENTEL	Wren Telephonist
WRENTSA	Wren Training Support Assistant
WRENWA	Wren Weapon Analyst
WRENWTR(G)	Wren Writer (General)
(P)	(Pay)
(S)	(Shorthand)
WRINS	Women's Royal Indian Naval Service
WRNR	West Riding National Reserve
	Women's Royal Naval Reserve
WRNS	Women's Royal Naval Service
WRNSR	Women's Royal Naval Service Reserve
WRNVR	Women's Royal Naval Volunteer Reserve
WRV	West Riding Volunteers
WS	War Substantive
WSC	Wilkinson Sword Company
WSCD	Welfare & Service Conditions Department
WSIY	West Somerset Imperial Yeomanry
WSO	Warrant Stores Officer
	WRAF Staff Officer
WSY	West Somerset Yeomanry

WSYC	West Somerset Yeomanry Cavalry
WT	Warrant Telegraphist
	War Transport
Wt	Watertight
W/T	Wireless Telegraphist
	Wireless Telegraphy
WTC	War Transport Council
WTD	War Trade Department
WTO	Wireless Telegraphy Officer
Wtr	Writer
WTS	Women's Transport Service
WVDF	Wolverhampton Volunteer Defence Force
WVEE	Wheeled Vehicles Experimental Establishment
WVR	Wakefield Volunteer Rifles
	Wellington Volunteer Rifles
	Women's Volunteer Reserve
WVRC	Wolverhampton Volunteer Rifle Corps
WW	Walking Wounded
	Warrant Writer
	Welfare Worker
WW I	World War One
WW II	World War Two
WWCP	Walking Wounded Collecting Post
WWCT Regt	Wellington West Coast & Taranaki Regiment
W Wdr	Warrant Wardmaster
WWO	Warrant Writer Officer
	Wing Warrant Officer
WWSA	Women's War Service Auxiliary
WWY	Warwickshire & Worcestershire Yeomanry
WY	Warwickshire Yeomanry
WYC	Warwickshire Yeomanry Cavalry
WYR	West Yorkshire Regiment
WYRV	West Yorkshire Rifle Volunteers
WYVR	West Yorkshire Volunteer Rifles
WYYC	West Yorkshire Yeomanry Cavalry
WZ	War Zone
X	eXercise
	eXperimental
	eXplosives
XRA	X-Ray Assistant
XX Committee	Doublecross Committee
Y	Yeomanry
YC	Yard Craft
	Yeomanry Cavalry

YCV	Young Citizens Volunteers (14th (Service) Battalion, Royal Irish Rifles)
YD	Yorkshire Dragoons
YE	Youth Entry
Ye Et Rg Rt	Yorkshire East Riding Regiment
Yeo	Yeomanry
Yeomy	Yeomanry
YH	Yorkshire Hussars
YHIY	Yorkshire Hussars Imperial Yeomanry
Y & L	York & Lancaster Regiment
YLI	Yorkshire Light Infantry
Y & L R	York & Lancaster Regiment
YO	Young Officer
YS	Yacht Service
	Young Soldier
YVT	Youth Visiting Team

Some Alternative & Unofficial Abbreviations

ACC	Army Criminal Corps
AFPU	Army Field Punishment Unit
Ammo	Ammunition
AOC	Angels of Christ
APM	A Permanent Malingerer
ASAP	As Soon As Possible
ASC	Ally Sloper's Cavalry
	Army Safety Corps
	Army Slop Corps
	Aunt Sally's Cavalry
BB	British Blues
BBB	Bigland's Birkenhead Bantams
	Burton's Bantam Battalion
BUMF	Bumfodder
CMAR	Can't Manage A Rifle (RAMC *reversed*)
DYF	Damned Young Fool
ELH	Egypt's Last Hope (*Grant tank*)
ENSA	Even NAAFI Stands Aghast
	Every Night Something Atrocious/Awful
ETB	Elastic Top & Bottom (WREN *knickers*)
FA	Fanny Adams
FIA	Forced Into Action (AIF *reversed*)
FUMTU	F – – ked Up More Than Usual
GSI	Got Some In Medal (1939–1945 *Star*)
HAC	Home And Colonial
HD	Harper's Duds
	Highway Decorators
IAMC	Idher Ao [Urdu – *come here*] Matron's Coming
IBA	Ignorant Bloody Aircrafthand
ID	Identity
IMFU	Imperial Military F – – k Up
IMS	Infinitely More So

JSC	Just Senior to Christ
KHB	King's Hard Bargain
KOB	Kokky-Olly Birds
KODR	King's Own Despatch Riders
K of K	Kitchener of Khartoum
KRRC	King's Rich Rude Rifles
LDV	Look, Duck, & Vanish
	Long-Dentured Veterans
LTC	London Thieving Corps
MC	Maconochie Cross
MFU	Military F – – k Up
MM	Maconochie Medal
MMS	Mickey Mouses
MRU	Much Regret Unable
MSSC	My Sister Sells Cabbages
MT	Moke Train
	Muck Train
	Murdering Thieves
MTF	Must Touch Flesh
NAAFI	No Aim, Ambition, or Further Interest
	No Ambition And Fractional Interest
	No Ambition And F – – kall Interest
NABU	Non-Adjustable Balls-Up
NBG	No Bloody Good
NCD	No Can Do
NQTD	Not Quite Top Drawer
NYD	Not Yet Dead
PBI	Poor Bloody Infantry
PBO	Poor Bloody Observer
PDQ	Pretty Damn Quick
PLU	People Like Us
psc	practically senior to Christ
PU	Pick-Up
RAMC	Rather A Mixed Crowd
	Rather A Moderate Corps
	Rats After Mouldy Cheese
	Rob All My Comrades
	Run Away Matron's Coming
RAOC	Rob All Our Comrades
RASC	Run Away Someone's Coming

REME	Rarely Electrically or Mechanically Efficient .
RHIP	Rank Hath Its Privileges
RIASC	Really I Am So Common
RNAS	Royal Nobs And Swankers
ROD	Roll on Demobilization
RPC	Request the Pleasure of your Company
SABU	Self-Adjusting Balls-Up
SEAC	Supreme Example of Allied Confusion
SNAFU	Situation Normal All F – – ked Up
SOS	Same Old Stew
SOB	Silly Old Blighter
SRD	Soon Run Dry
S & T Corps	Sausage and Tumtum [*native cart*] Corps
TABU	Typical Army Balls-Up
TARFU	Things Are Really F – – ked Up
TG	Temporary Gentleman
TOG	The Old Gang
VAD	Very Able Darlings
	Very Adaptable Dames
	Very Attractive Damsels
	Virgins Almost Desperate
	Virtuous And Dependable
	Vivacious And Delicious
VMT	Very Many Thanks
WMP	With Much Pleasure
WRAC	Weekly Ration of Army C – – t
Y & L	Young & Lovelies

REME	Rarely Electrocalls by Mechanically Efficient
RHIP	Rank Hath Its Privileges
RIASC	Really I Am So Common
RNAS	Royal Nobs And Snarkers
ROD	Roll on D-mobilisation
RPC	Request the Pleasure of your Company

S/RE	Self-Adjusting Rall-Up
SEAC	Supreme Example of Allied Confusion
SNAFU	Situation Normal All F---ked Up
SOS	Same Old Stew
SOB	Silly Old Bugher
SRD	Soon Run Dry
S & T Corps	Sausage and Tomato leave zero Chips

FARU	Typical Army Ball-Up
TARFU	Things Are Really F---ked Up
TG	Temporary Gentleman
TOG	The Old Gang

VAD	Very Able Darlings
	Very Adaptable Dames
	Very Attractive Damsels
	Virgins Almost Desperate
	Various And Dependable
	Vivacious And Delicious
VMT	Very Many Thanks

| WMP | With Much Pleasure |
| WRAC | Weekly Ration of Army C---? |

| Y & L | Young & Lovelies |